From the Files of MCC

The
Mennonite Central Committee
Story Series

The Mennonite Central Committee Story
Volume 1. Documents

From the Files of MCC

Cornelius J. Dyck, Editor
With Robert S. Kreider and John A. Lapp

HERALD PRESS
Scottdale, Pennsylvania
Kitchener, Ontario
1980

Library of Congress Cataloging in Publication Data

Main entry under title:
The Mennonite Central Committee story.
    CONTENTS: v. 1. From the files of MCC.—
v. 2. Responding to worldwide needs.—v. 3.
Witness and service in North America.
    1. Mennonite Central Committee—History—
Sources. 2. Mennonites—Charities—History—
Sources. I. Dyck, Cornelius J. II. Kreider,
Robert S. III. Lapp, John Allen. IV. Mennonite
Central Committee.
BX8128.W4M46   361.7'5   80-10975
ISBN 0-8361-1229-6 (v. 1)
ISBN 0-8361-1230-X (v. 2)
ISBN 0-8361-1231-8 (v. 3)

Contents

Preface

When the idea of writing a history of the Mennonite Central Committee (MCC) was first raised with several of us who have been close to its life and work our response was not positive. Who would read a big volume about an agency that has become an institution and is simply taken for granted among Mennonites, and perhaps others? Besides, we do have A Ministry of Goodwill. A Short Account of Mennonite Relief, 1939-1949, written by Irvin B. Horst, (Akron, 1950), and the larger volume In The Name of Christ, by John D. Unruh (Scottdale, 1952), as well as other writings about the life and work of MCC. There seemed to be no shortage of available information.

In reflecting further on the question, however, it became clear to us that most of this literature was <u>about</u> MCC and that the readers had little opportunity to see for themselves how MCC worked, how its decisions were made, or how it all began. And so a proposal grew among us for the preparation of several smaller volumes which would tell the MCC · story in a first-hand way and become a resource for other writers, for study groups in congregations and schools, as well as for private enjoyment.

For the present this has led to the preparation of five modest volumes, with the possibility of one or two more being added later. Of these five the first three form a unit which might simply be called "From the Files of the MCC", volume four contains the biographies of fifteen persons and, in some cases, spouses who have played a central role in MCC over many years, and volume five, which is still in preparation, might be called "What would you do if...?" because it presents specific situations from MCC experiences around the world in terms of crucial ethical and other issues and choices faced by MCC persons in their ministries.

The decisions about what and whom to include were difficult. In the first three volumes the rows of file boxes filled with interesting documents were almost overwhelming. Only a few could be selected, hopefully representative of the issues considered, and placed into context by brief introductory notations. <u>Spelling and punctuation errors in the documents have been left as they were and have not been identified with the standard /sic/ to avoid excessive cluttering up of the manuscripts.</u> Whom to include in a small collection of biographies proved equally difficult. It is hoped that it may

become possible to compile another volume eventually of the
great contributions made to MCC by non-North Americans. Only
two of these biographies are included in volume four. The
selection of issues and choices faced in sixty years of global activities was equally difficult, from the death of Clayton
Kratz in Russia in 1920 to the involvement in Vietnam in the
1960s and 70s. To ask "What would you do..." in specific
difficult situations can lead to spiritual growth and, perhaps,
to words of counsel to MCC and persons serving with it.

The primary committee appointed by the MCC Executive
Committee to guide this project consisted of Robert S. Kreider
of Bethel College, North Newton, Kansas, John A. Lapp of Goshen
College, Goshen, Indiana, and Cornelius J. Dyck of the Associated Mennonite Biblical Seminaries, Elkhart, Indiana who, in
his capacity as Director of the Institute of Mennonite Studies
was responsible for the implementation of the project. His
debt to the wisdom and help of the other two members of the
committee is here gratefully acknowledged. A larger committee
was convened once for consultation, but written counsel was
also received and appreciated. Its members were Paul Longacre
and William T. Snyder of MCC, to whom special recognition is
due for their strong support and encouragement, but also to
Clarence Hiebert of Tabor College, Kenneth B. Hoover of Messiah
College, J. M. Klassen and Dan Zehr of MCC (Canada), and Ted D.
Regehr of Saskatoon, Saskatchewan.

Beyond these recognitions deep appreciation is expressed
here to the many others who helped in one way or another, including Vernon Neufeld of Mennonite Mental Health Services
for facilitating the selection of documents in that field, to
Leonard Gross and Sharon Klingelsmith of the Archives of the
Mennonite Church at Goshen, to typists and researchers Lois
Janzen, Jennifer L. Dyck, Shirley B. Souder and particularly
to Suzanne Keeney Lind and Sue Yoder for exceptional skills
in research and in typing respectively. The writers of the
biographies deserve their own special praise for erecting
monuments in tribute to those whose lives they shared with us.
The project could not have been undertaken without the financial
and moral support of the MCC itself, through its Executive
Committee and Annual Meeting, which is here gratefully acknowledged.

May all that has been done be "In The Name Of Christ",
in His Spirit, and to His honor and glory.

Cornelius J. Dyck, Director
Institute of Mennonite Studies
June, 1979

1.
How the MCC Began

The Mennonite Central Committee was organized in response to the needs caused by World War I and, more specifically, in response to the plight of the Mennonites in Russia in the early 1920's.

Several Mennonite groups already had functioning relief committees: "The Emergency Relief Commission of the General Conference Mennonite Church had been made a standing body as early as 1899, prompted largely by the severe famine conditions in India. The Mennonite Brethren Church had been channeling its relief work through its Board of Foreign Missions. The (old) Mennonites had launched their Relief Commission for War Sufferers in December, 1917. Through these channels the Mennonites out of their abundance shared with the victims of war in various countries in Europe...

"...In response to the urgent request for help in the Mennonite communities of Siberia, Mennonites on the /Pacific/ coast collected large quantities of new and used clothing. Due to the large amount collected it was considered wise to let M. B. Fast accompany the shipment which was sent in 1919...

"...Fast's/ vivid reports and urgent appeals led to the formation on January 4, 1920, of the Emergency Relief Committee of the Mennonites of North America...

"This committee, however, soon found the door to Siberia closed and so concentrated its attention on Central Europe. When later in the same year (1920) the Mennonite Central Committee was organized, the Emergency Relief Committee agreed to cooperate in the new framework and asked its chairman, P. C. Hiebert, to represent it in the new central committee.

"It will thus be seen that when the Studien-Kommission came to America to bring news of the Russian situation, American Mennonites were already active. There was no channel, however, through which all activities could be centralized..." John D. Unruh, In the Name of Christ - A History of the Mennonite Central Committee and Its Service 1920-1951. (Scottdale: Herald Press, 1952), pp. 5-6.

Reading 1
P. C. Hiebert, Feeding the Hungry: Russia Famine, 1919-1925 (Scottdale: MCC, 1929).

For centuries Mennonites have generally been acknowledged to be a thrifty, well-to-do people, who provided for
their own poor, of whom they usually had but few. They
also have the reputation of being peace-loving and law-
abiding. They have, however, often been charged with being
rather self-centered and manifesting but a limited interest
in things outside of their circles.

At various times leaders of vision have urged them to
reach out farther, in an effort to help the needy and to
give the world the Gospel; yet little progress was made in
this matter until a vital impetus was given to this work by
a great famine of India in 1899, when several groups of
Mennonites sent representatives with food to minister to the
physical and the spiritual needs of the people. Out of
these and later efforts, have developed several of the pres-
ent-day missionary enterprises of the Mennonites in foreign
lands.

Soon after the beginning of the /first/ World War a
plea for help came to America from the starving in Belgium
and northern France. In response the Mennonites gave freely.
As the war continued, this need broadened and gave the Mennonites an opportunity to relieve much suffering in France,
Germany, Austria, and Poland. During this time the Mennonites contributed large sums of money to the cause of relief,
and a number of their young men volunteered for service
among the needy of Europe and Asia /working mainly with the
American Red Cross, American Friends Service Committee, and
Near East Relief/. (p. 27)

But it was felt that more effective work could be done,
and more interest could be aroused among the Mennonite constituency, if an independent task would be undertaken by
them. At first there seemed to be no satisfactory opening,
but the various fields were watched, and finally sentiment
crystallized on the idea that Russia was the field for the
American Mennonite Church. (p. 29)

The first authentic and direct information from Russia
was brought by the "Studien Kommission" consisting of the
four delegates of the Russian brethren to the outside world,
namely Benj. Unruh and A. A. Friesen of Halbstadt, K. H.
Warkentin, Waldheim and John Esau, of Ekaterinanslaw, South
Russia. These awakened the American Mennonites to the realization of the dire need of their brethren abroad, and showed
them their duty of giving material aid to an extent that they
had not thought possible. (p. 31)

Upon the solicitation of /the Studien Kommission/ an
informal meeting of the various branches of the Mennonites
in the Central States was called for July 13th, 1920, to
meet at Newton, Kansas, to listen to the report of the needs
in Russia and to discuss ways and means of sending help. To

a fair representation of Mennonites from Kansas and Oklahoma, the delegates gave their report and also expressed their request for relief in a larger united effort of the Mennonites of America. After considerable discussion, a Committee on Information was appointed, whose business should be to secure data that would facilitate the preparation of some feasible plan for aiding in emigrating from the land which could no more be their home under prevailing social and political conditions. The Committee thus appointed consisted of the following five brethren: D. H. Bender, Hesston, Kans,; John Lichti, Medford, Okla.; W. J. Ewert, Hillsboro, Kans.; P. C. Hiebert, Hillsboro, Kans.; and D. E. Harder, Hillsboro, Kans. This committee of five organized with W. J. Ewert as Chairman and P. C. Hiebert as Secretary. At their meeting in Hillsboro, Kans., at the home of Bro. Hiebert on July 19 and 20, after much deliberation on the scope of their work and questions relating thereto, it was agreed that a joint meeting of representatives of Mennonite Relief Organizations should be called to meet at Elkhart, Indiana on the 27th day of July, 1920. Bro. D. H. Bender was entrusted with the duty of sending out the formal call in the name of the Committee on Information. (pp. 48-49)

*   *   *

The following report on the work of the Mennonite Relief Commission for War Sufferers outlines the activities of one of the independent Mennonite relief organizations before the formation of the Central Committee. The MCC's first major project, the Constantinople unit and Russian relief originated in this Commission.

Reading 2
Report of Mennonite Relief Commission for War Sufferers, probably written in July 1920.

A synopsis of the work done and present plans for Russian relief may be of interest to many. The work that has been done by the Mennonite Relief Commission for War Sufferers has been largely as a foundation to get our organizations, in line for some recognized work distinctive as a Mennonite organization. At the time the Commission was organized /1917/, it was the fond hope of many that ways and means could be provided whereby men could be sent on the field to distribute the gifts received. At that time, while the war was in progress, it was found impossible to do so. Later, however, avenues were found through which we could send men under the direction of other organizations. This opportunity was used for the time being, and a number of men went to France to help in reconstruction work under

the direction of the American Friends Service Committee.
This privilege was highly appreciated, but it did not meet
the original idea of the Commission.

After the signing of the Armistice, a new field of
operation was opened in the Near East. Steps were taken to
enter this field and a group of seven workers, with two
others to make a survey of conditions, were sent with the
second relief transport sent out by the American Committee
for Armenian and Syrian Relief which organization is now
called the Near East Relief. Our relations with this organization have been very satisfactory. We found, however,
after reaching the field, that it was not advisable to take
up the work as a separate unit and our men were assigned to
responsible positions throughout the Syrian district in
connection with the general work. Additional workers were
sent to the field, and after the term of service for the
first group had expired new men were sent to take their
places.

While engaged in the two projects above named, Germany
was opened for relief work and Austria as well. Our attention
had also been directed to Russia, largely no doubt because
of the vastness of the field and the apparent need as reported from various sources. The fact that there were many
Mennonites living there also had due consideration.

About Sept. 1, 1919 the first step was taken to enter
these fields. A committee of three Mennonite workers in
France was commissioned to make an investigating tour through
central Europe and to proceed to Russia if possible. The
committee appointed was J. R. Allgyer, A. J. Miller, and
A. E. Hiebert. They immediately gave their attention to
their new task. Their first report came from Vienna, Austria,
after having spent some time in Germany and a few days in
that city. The conditions of these two countries were set
forth and an appeal made for help if possible. A. E. Hiebert
remained here while the other two of the committee continued
their tour through Zecho-Slavika, Roumania, and the southern
part of the Ukraine. On their return to France, J. R. Allgyer
returned to America and brought their report to the Commission,
a report of which has been circulated in our periodicals.

Since that time an avenue was opened to do relief work
in Germany through the Mennonites located there. Funds have
been contributed and forwarded to the Mennonite Commission
operating there, which is a local organization. Funds have
also been contributed and forwarded to Vienna for the work
done their through the American Friends Service Committee.

Our attention has been given more directly, however, to
the opening of some definite relief work in Russia. At one
time it was thought possible to enter the country with an

abundant supply of relief commodities to be given by the
Ukrainian Commission. These supplies had been located in
France and were supposed to be available for this work. It
later developed that the supplies could not be secured and
the matter was dropped.

The next development in the Russian proposition was in
the form of a cablegram received from A. J. Miller, a member
of our committee and who had remained at Paris. His cablegram indicated that it would be possible to open work in
Sebastapol and there was an abundant store of supplies
available at Constantinople. The Red Cross officials at
Washington, however, could not give us any encouragement
along this line.

Our final solution of the matter was reached about
June 20, 1920, at which time an arrangement was effected
with the Near East Relief, New York City, through which
we were encouraged to send a group of workers to Constantinople. This group should carry letters of recommendation
to the main office of the Near East Relief at Constantinople
and they in consultation should decide on the kind of work
our men should do in case the way to enter Russia should
be closed for the time being. By so doing, our group would
be in readiness to move on at the first opportunity to enter
that country. The Near East Relief has offered to render all
assistance possible in the securing of passports for our men,
a matter which is of special importance as the government
officials at Washington are very particular as to who is
allowed to go to Constantinople and how long they shall remain, transmission of our money, transportation of clothing
and supplies, securing of passage for our groups, etc. This
generous offer from the Near East Relief is only a continuance
of the congenial relations existing with our organization
and our men on the field.

On the strength of the above opportunity we immediately
set ourselves to the task of securing our group of men to go.
The first requirement was to have someone direct the opening
of the work who had been on the field under the Near East
Relief. Orie O. Miller, Akron, Pa., was appointed to fill
this place. Two other workers have been appointed to accompany him. Others are arranging to follow later. Many details
accompany a project of this kind, but it is now planned to
have the first group sail September 1.

A budget of $10,000 per month for August and September
has been allowed for this work. The amount allowed for
August will be expended here for the collecting and forwarding of a small shipment of used clothing, some new clothing, hospital supplies, and the outfitting and paying of
passage for the group. The September budget will be taken
to Constantinople.

We are not attempting to say how soon our group can enter Russia. This however is our final purpose. If there should be any delay, the work that we propose to do among the Russian refugees gathered near Constantinople will be worthy of our consideration and ought to be valuable to us later. Our group sailing Sept. 1 will be instructed to keep us informed relative to the work and this information will be made public from time to time.

We are glad for the prospect of having a generous co-operation from the different Mennonite Relief Commissions and Conferences in this work. Encouraging reports are coming to us from different sections and we hope to announce shortly that the organization of the Mennonite Central Committee has been completed. In the mean time contributions for the work can be forwarded to the respective organizations of each branch of Mennonites as heretofore. Each Commission will continue to receive money and the Committee is a means to bring the funds together under one common head for distribution on the field.

Levi Mumaw, Secretary

*   *   *

The meetings held on July 27 and 28, 1920, were mainly concerned with the immediate problem of aid to Russia (Reading 3 and 4, The Gospel Herald (XIII:21), August 19, 1920). The first organizational and functional meeting of of the Mennonite Central Committee was held on September 27, 1920 (Reading 5, The Gospel Herald (XIII:28), October 7, 1920).

Reading 3

Report Of the Joint Meeting of the Mennonite Relief Committees, Elkhart, Ind., July 27, 1920.

For the Gospel Herald

1. The meeting was opened by prayer and Scripture reading by D. D. Miller, Middlebury, Ind.

2. The organization of the joint committee was effected by elected the following officers: Mod., D. H. Bender, Hesston, Kans.; Secy., P. C. Hiebert, Hillsboro, Kans.

3. A public meeting for the evening was agreed upon for the purpose of hearing a report on the conditions in S. Russia, by A. A. Friesen, Halbstadt, S. Russia.

4. Aaron Loucks, Scottdale, Pa., explained his purpose in requesting this meeting to be called in the following:

a. The Mennonite Relief Commission for War Sufferers expects to send a unit of relief workers to S. Russia in the month of August. The Russian Committee had desired this meeting of all the relief committees to accord to all an opportunity for co-operation.

b. The Relief Commission also expects to make a shipment of supplies accompanied by two brethren, and there is room for a third party.

5. H. H. Regier, Mountain Lake, Minn., who had been designated by the Relief Com. of the General Conference of Mennonites, reports that he has been refused a passport, which precludes his going. It is suggested that he secure a passport to Constantinople, and from there travel on a visa from the American consul.

6. It was further suggested that the services of the Near East Relief Commission be engaged to secure passport.

7. The advisability of sending workers to Russia at this time was questioned, and answered by the response that advance workers are now being sent to open the field for others following later.

8. A. A. Friesen explained conditions in S. Russia bearing on the question of relief at this time.

a. The field and the need is very extensive. 100,000 Mennonites and many Lutheran and Catholic colonists surround them. The greatest needs today are: clothing, medicines, foods, etc. Such as can should be encouraged to pay for what they receive; others must be helped outright.

b. The work of distribution should be carried out in united action by all the relief workers. Several very definite advantages appear therein.

c. For America the several standing Relief Committees might continue, but it is advisable that they have a joint executive committee.

8. Meeting dismissed with prayer by Wm. J. Ewert, Hillsboro, Kans.

Second Session. 1.00 P.M.

1. The question of organizing for united relief work was discussed, several plans being suggested, which resulted in the following resolution being passed:

Resolved, that we, the representatives of the several branches of Mennonites assembled at Elkhart, Ind., this 27th day of July, 1920, deem it well and desirable to create a Mennonite Central Committee, whose duty shall be to function with and for the several relief committees of the Mennonites in taking charge of all gifts for S. Russia, to make all purchases of suitable articles for relief work, and to provide for the transportation and the equitable distribution of the same.

2. Pertaining to the methods of securing the above named Central Committee the following agreement was reached:

Resolved, that this Mennonite Central Committee shall

consist of not more than one member from each Mennonite relief commission that wishes to co-operate in this work for
S. Russia.

   3.   It was further Resolved, that the following form
the temporary body of the Mennonite Central Committee:
      Levi Mumaw, Scottdale, Pa., for the Mennonites.

   H. H. Regier, Mt. Lake, Minn., for the General Conference Mennonites.

   P. C. Hiebert, Hillsboro, Kans., for the Mennonite
Brethren.

   4.   After instructing this committee to effect a temporary organization and to draw up a tentative plan of co-
operation, the meeting adjourned to meet again at 6:02 P.M.

Evening Session
(Immigration and Emigration Questions)
   1.   A. A. Friesen, Halbstadt, S. Russia, in presenting
the problem, called attention to the following issues involved:
   a.   Emigration may involve difficulties that may need
diplomatic operation or influence from the American Government.

   b.   It may be necessary that the American Mennonites
go on bond for their Russian brethren to insure their admission into this country.

   c.   The Russian Mennonites do not need nor wish gifts,
but rather loans, which they hope to pay off in full in due
time.

   d.   We need an organization to direct the reception of
the Mennonite immigrants to this country and to assist in
getting them located in their future homes.

   f.   An organization to take charge of the finances of
the immigrants would be very desirable.

   The following names were mentioned in connection with
the projected finance committee: Maxwell H. Kratz, Philadelphia, Pa.; Peter Janzen, Beatrice, Nebr.; Joseph Bechtel,
Philadelphia, Pa.; Wm. A. Derstine, Quakertown, Pa.; Alfred G.
Scattergood, Philadelphia, Pa.

   p.   The advisability of calling a general conference
of all the Mennonites in America was considered, during the
remainder of the session.   Thereupon followed adjournment
until 8:32 A.M., July 28

Fourth Session, July 28
   1.   Meeting was opened by prayer led by Levi Mumaw.
   2.   General conference question continued, and ended
by the meeting passing the following resolution:
   Resolved, that it be declared the sense of this meeting,
that we favor the plan of having each conference appoint a

representative, these together to compose a representative body, who are to organize an executive committee, whose duty it shall be to consider and execute any work that may arise in connection with the proposed immigration of Russian Mennonites. Be it further

Resolved, that a committee of three be appointed to work out the details necessary to perfect and carry out the above plan.

3. The following persons were appointed on this committee: S. C. Yoder, Kalona, Iowa; Wm. J. Ewert, Hillsboro, Kans.; P. C. Hiebert, Hillsboro, Kans.

4. After a short recess the committee reported as follows:

Report of the committee on resolutions.

In view of the fact that our brethren in S. Russia have suffered untold hardships as a result of the war, and as a result are now almost in destitution; and on account of the unsettled condition of the country it is now impossible to live there with any assurance of security to life and property,--Therefore, we, the undersigned, representing different branches of the Mennonite Church, assembled in session at Elkhart, Ind., July 27, 28, 1920, submit the following recommendations to our respective conferences for approval:

We recommend that an executive committee consisting of five members be appointed to co-operate with our Russian brethren in working out plans with our government, means of financing the undertaking, and render such assistance as may be needed in connection with the movement.

Manner of Appointment. We recommend that each conference appoint a representative to meet at such time and place as hereinafter provided for, for the purpose of selecting the aforesaid Executive Committee. We further recommend, that in case conferences have held their session for the year, that the Executive Committees or the proper officials of the same be notified and that these then act for their conference.

Presentation to Conferences. We recommend that the members of the respective Mennonite churches here represented get together and decide who is to present these resolutions to the conferences, and that the secretary of this meeting be instructed to write to the proper officials of conferences not represented here asking them to present these recommendations to their conferences for approval or action. In case these recommendations are not fully understood, they shall have the privilege of calling on one of the undersigned for help.

Organization of Conference Representatives. We further recommend that as soon as possible after conferences, and

executive committees of same where such have been required
to act for their conferences, have acted on these recommendations the result of same be transmitted to P. C. Hiebert,
Hillsboro, Kans., secretary of the Committee on Information,
and on receipt of this information Wm. J. Ewert, of Hillsboro,
Kans., Chairman of the Committee on Information, shall call
a meeting of these delegates at such time and place as the
Committee on Information shall deem suitable.

An Appeal to the Brotherhood. The report of the brethren
who have come from the stricken country is a touching one,
and presents to us a great need of such propositions that
merits the co-operation of every one of the brotherhood in
the U.S. The physical suffering, mental anguish, together
with the destitution of the means of subsistence makes it
imperative that we take concerted action at the earliest
possible time to help them in their distress. We trust
that the brotherhood, which has always rallied to the assistance of the needy when their cry has reached them, will not
neglect this opportunity of rendering help to those who are
of the "Household of Faith." We urge that our conferences
take action as soon as possible and that those who are responsible for transmitting the reports to the secretary will
do so without delay, that the work may be taken up in an
authoritative manner at the earliest possible time. Thanking
the brotherhood for their responses to the recommendations
of unofficial bodies in the past, and trusting that in this
time of distress and pressing need you will give us the aid
to provide for the work as herein set forth, we beg to remain,

Your humble servants.
D. H. Bender, Hesston, Kans.
H. H. Regier, Mt. Lake, Minn.
Wm. J. Ewert, Hillsboro, Kans.
D. D. Miller, Middlebury, Ind.
V. E. Reiff, Elkhart, Ind.
S. C. Yoder, Kalona, Iowa.
Orie O. Miller, Akron, Pa.
Aaron Loucks, Scottdale, Pa.
P. C. Hiebert, Hillsboro, Kans.
Vernon Smucker, Scottdale, Pa.
Ernest Miller, Rawson, Ohio.
Eli G. Reist, Mount Joy, Pa.
Levi Mumaw, Scottdale, Pa.

This report was accepted by the delegates and officially
signed by each member present.

5.   The Mennonite Central Committee gave a report of

the work done at a session held before the opening of the
joint meeting. The report was accepted as read.

Reading 4
Minutes of Meeting of the Mennonite Central Committee

In accordance with action taken at a meeting of several
Mennonite Relief Commissions held July 26 and 28, 1920, creating
and authorizing this Committee for action in connection with
the proposed Russian Relief work, a meeting was held at the
Mennonite Meeting House in Elkhart, Ind., July 28, 1920.

The following members were present: H. H. Regier, Mt.
Lake, Minn., Levi Mumaw, Scottdale, Pa., and P. C. Hiebert,
Hillsboro, Kans. These members had been selected temporarily
at the said joint meeting to serve until a permanent committee
is elected.

The committee agreed to organize on the basis of the
following motion:

Resolved: That the committee organize with a chairman
and secretary-treasurer, it being understood that the secretary-treasurer be the active member of the committee.

The provisional organization resulted as follows:
P. C. Hiebert, chairman; Levi Mumaw, secretary-treasurer.

The following action was taken:

1. Resolved: That the secretary-treasurer be instructed
to communicate with each Mennonite relief commission or conference anticipating to co-operate in Russian relief work,
giving information concerning the work done thus far and
the further purpose and plans of the committee and to invite
them to elect their member to serve on the Mennonite Central
Committee.

2. Resolved; That the following organizations be
placed on our list:

(a) Mennonite Relief Commission for War Sufferers,
Levi Mumaw, Secretary, Scottdale, Pa. Official organ--
"Gospel Herald," Scottdale, Pa.

(b) Emergency Relief Committee of the General Conference,
John Lichti, Secretary, Deer Creek, Okla. Official organ--
"Bundesbote," Berne, Ind.

(c) The Emergency Relief Committee of the Mennonites
of North America, D. E. Harder, Secretary, Hillsboro, Kans.

(d) Relief Commission of the Central Conference of
Illinois Mennonites, Val. Strubhar, Secretary, Washington,
Ill. Official organ--"Christian Evangel."

(e) Mennonite Brethren Church of North America, P. C.
Hiebert, Hillsboro, Kans. Official organ--"Zionsbote,"
Hillsboro. Kans.

(f) Krimmer Mennonite Brethren, D. M. Hofer, Chicago,
Ill. Official organ--"Wahrheitsfreund", Chicago, Ill.

3. Resolved, That a meeting be called for the purpose
of permanent organization and the initiation of the regular
work as soon as returns have been received and it is deemed
advisable by the temporary officers of the committee.

4. Resolved, That the space of the meeting be determined by the temporary officers of the committee.

5. Resolved, That the secretary-treasurer be instructed
to keep accurate accounts of all expenses in connection with
the work of the committee.

6. Resolved, That the report of this meeting be
published in the official organs of the dicerent organizations
with a synopsis of the history and present status of the
Russian Work.

Adjournment.

Levi Mumaw, Secretary-Treasurer.

P.S. The above action was later approved by the joint
meeting of the Relief Commissions held the same day.

The meeting adjourned.

P. C. Hiebert, Secretary.

Reading 5
Minutes of Meeting of Mennonite Central Committee

Held at Chicago, Ill., Sept. 27, 1920.

Pursuant to the call of the Chairman, the first meeting
of the Mennonite Central Committee was held at 2812 Lincoln
Ave., Chicago, Ill. The Chairman, P. C. Hiebert called the
meeting to order at 10:30 A.M. The following members were
present: P. C. Hiebert, J. H. Mellinger, D. M. Hofer, M. H.
Kratz, and Levi Mumaw.

D. M. Hofer led a short devotional service.

The minutes of the preliminary meeting held at Elkhart,
Ind., July 28, 1920, were read and accepted.

It was moved and supported that we elect a Chairman,
Secretary-Treasurer and a Third Member to constitute an Executive Committee of the Mennonite Central Committee. The
Secretary-Treasurer also to act as Executive Secretary for
the Committee. Carried unanimously.

The election of officers resulted as follows:

Chairman, P. C. Hiebert, Hillsboro, Kans.; Secretary-
Treasurer, Levi Mumaw, Scottdale, Pa.; Third Member, Maxwell
H. Kratz, 1137 Commercial Trust Building, Philadelphia, Pa.

The following action was taken:

Resolved; That we accept our duties as Mennonite Central
Committee as outlined by a resolution passed at the meeting
of the different organizations at Elkhart, Ind., July 27-28,
1920, calling this Committee into existence--"that we, the
representatives of the several branches of Mennonites assembled
at Elkhart, Ind., this 27th day of July, 1920, deem it well

and desirable to create a Mennonite Central Committee whose
duty it shall be to function with and for the several relief
committees of the Mennonites in taking charge of all gifts
for South Russia, to make all purchases of suitable articles
for relief work, and to provide for the transportation and
the equitable distribution of the same."

Resolved; That the Chairman and Secretary-Treasurer be
appointed a committee of two to submit an outline as to the
procedure of the Committee in the forwarding and distribution
of funds and materials.

The committee submitted the following:

Resolved; That we accept the plans now in force and
adopted by the Mennonite Relief Commission and the group of
workers reaching Constantinople on this date, which read as
follows:

Pertaining to Finances

1. That the unit on the field be allowed a definite
monthly budget for relief expenditure, and that the Director
be notified of the amount authorized at least two months in
advance.

2. That the Director of the Unit issue receipt of all
amounts forwarded to him on the field, that he be held responsible for a careful accounting of these funds to the
Treasurer of the Commission, that in as far as possible such
accounts be covered by signed vouchers indicating the final
disposition of these funds.

3. That all personnel, travel and maintenance expense
accounts on the field be O. K.'d by the Director before being
paid by the Treasurer of the unit.

4. That a monthly report of all field expenditures be
made to the Treasurer of the Commission.

5. That the Publicity Committee, subject to the approval
of the Chairman of the Executive Committee, be authorized to
actively carry on publicity work in connection with the Russian proposition for purpose of raising funds to carry on the
work, but that all expenditures for purpose of publishing,
literature, pamphlets or in travel be approved by the Executive Committee.

Pertaining to Work on the Field

1. That all work on the field be under the charge of
one Director who shall be appointed or his appointment be
approved by the Relief Commission. He is to be the medium of
all official relations between the unit and the Commission,
and be empowered to act for the Commission in any official
capacity on the field. He assigns personnel, is finally responsible for the adoption of any field policies of work,
selects and recommends to the Commission for appointment any

new personnel who may be procured·on the field.

2. That the unit be empowered to purchase any necessary equipment for the conduct of the work, but that any purchase of this nature be fully reported to the Commission at the end of each month, and that full inventory of equipment on hand be taken and reported at the end of each six month period.

3. That the unit use their best judgment in making grants of money or supplies to any other relief organization in a cooperative way.

4. That orphanage work may be opened on the field if such seems needed and advisable, but if adopted, definite plans as to the size of such work and its nature be submitted by the Unit to the Commission for approval as early as possible.

5. That monthly reports be made to the Commission of all work done including statistics of needy helped, etc.

The resolution was adopted and the plans accepted subject to change if found so necessary.

It was moved and supported that official information be sent regularly to each official organ of the several bodies represented and to each member of the Committee. The information to the papers to be sent in the language used by each. The motion was adopted unanimously.

Resolved: That D. M. Hofer, Vernon Smucker and the Secretary-Treasurer of the Committee constitute a Publicity Committee.

Resolved: That the expenses of the Mennonite Central Committee and its meetings be paid out of the funds and charged up as such.

Resolved: That meetings of the Mennonite Central Committee be called by the Executive Committee when necessary but if possible not over four times a year at such a time and place as may be considered best.

Adjournment.

Levi Mumaw, Sec'y-Treas.

2.
Relief and
Refugee Work in Russia

On September 2, 1920, Orie Miller, Akron, Pennsylvania; Arthur Slagel, Flanagan, Illinois; and Clayton Kratz, Perkasie, Pennsylvania, left for Constantinople. Their departure was reported in the Gospel Herald as follows:

Reading 6
The Gospel Herald (XIII:24), September 9, 1920.

On Wednesday afternoon, Sept. 1, at 4:30 o'clock, the steamship "Providence" sailed out of New York harbor, bound for Naples, Italy. This in itself would not deserve notice in these columns were it not for the fact that on this boat were three of our brethren, Miller, Slagel and Kratz, bound for South Russia via Constantinople and composing the first independent war relief unit ever sent out by the Mennonite Church. Many and difficult problems lie before them, and many are the prayers from the Church in America that will ascend in their behalf, both that they may have wisdom in meeting and solving the difficulties and problems which they will be called on to meet and in behalf of their protection and safe return. We especially call your attention to the farewell message written by Brother Miller just before sailing. Let us think of them often during the next few months.

Orie Miller's farewell message:

The good-byes have nearly all been given. Bro. Mumaw, Elta and Clarence Hess are still with us. The "Providence" is scheduled to leave port at 3 P.M. today, after which the home folks and home land will rapidly be left behind.

Brethren Slagel and Kratz unite with me in expressing our deepest appreciation of the interest shown by the Church in us and the work to which we have felt ourselves called. Our desire is to represent in all our work and labors the interests and principles of our Church in the most effective way, and likewise minister to those who are cold, sick and suffering in the country to which we are going. To this end we wish your prayers, your sympathies and support, suggestions and criticisms. Our address for the present time is c. o. Near East Relief, Constantinople, Turkey.

A constant effort will be made to keep the home people informed in a clear understandable way of disposition being

made of your money and clothes. Think of us as your servants
in their distribution that all may be done to His honor.
Orie Miller

*   *   *

This group arrived in Constantinople on September 27;
Miller and Kratz proceded directly to Russia, where they
visited Mennonite villages and made plans for a relief program. The Mennozentrum, a body representing all Russian
Mennonites, sent the following letter to the Central Committee in America.

Reading 7
The Gospel Herald (XIII:38), December 16, 1920.

TO THE CENTRAL COMMITTEE OF THE MENNONITES OF AMERICA

The Mennozentrum had the satisfaction in today's session to welcome the delegates of the American Mennonite
churches, the brethren, Orie Miller and C. H. Kratz who informed us concerning the extensive work for the relief of
the needy which has been carried on for some time by our
American brethren in other countries and is now about to
be undertaken in Russia. We have with sincere joy learned
of this noble work and it affords us satisfaction to know
that those of the same household of faith in America have
not forgotten us but are remembering us in brotherly love,
and that they take our need to heart. We hope and desire
that by means of this relief work the bonds which unite us
may be strengthened and brotherly love increased.
In the name of the Mennonite churches of South Russia
we express to the Mennonite churches in America our heart-
felt thanks for the noble work of mercy which they have
undertaken, and we send to the churches in the distant
country our greetings of love and best wishes. May God
add His blessing to the praiseworthy work and richly reward
the givers.

First Chairman of the Mennozentrum: Heinrich Schroder
Second Chairman: K. A. Wiens
Secretary: Peter Brann
Dated: Temporary Office of the general Mennonite organi-
zation "Mennozentrum," September 30 (October 13), 1920.

*   *   *

Developments in the civil war, however, prevented further relief work until the following year. Clayton Kratz,
who remained in a battle area, disappeared and was never
heard from again. Miller returned to Constantinople, where

relief efforts were concentrated until Alvin J. Miller received permission from the Russian authorities in August 1921, to begin a relief program in Russia.

On October 1, 1921, the contract between the Russian Socialist Federative Soviet Republic and the American Mennonite Relief was signed by Lev Kamenev on behalf of the Central Commission for Combatting Famine, or the All-Russia Central Executive Committee of the Soviets, and Alvin J. Miller as Director of the American Mennonite Relief, representing the Mennonite Central Committee. The following is an Appendix to that Agreement relating to agricultural reconstruction work.

Reading 8
Agricultural Reconstruction Agreement--Appendix to Agreement between American Mennonite Relief and Russian Socialist Federative Soviet Republic dated October 1, 1921.

APPENDIX
To Agreement between AMERICAN MENNONITE RELIEF and RUSSIAN SOCIALIST FEDERATIVE SOVIET REPUBLIC dated October 1, 1921.
AGRICULTURAL RECONSTRUCTION AGREEMENT

WHEREAS the American Mennonite Relief, an unofficial, volunteer, American organization for Christian social service, is now operating in Soviet Russia under an agreement entered into with the Russian Socialistic Federative Soviet Republic, which covers conditions under which the American Mennonite Relief is now rendering aid to the famine sufferers in Soviet Russia, and

WHEREAS it is desirable not only to relieve those suffering from famine but also to remove the causes of famine conditions and as fully as possible to prevent their recurrence by enabling the farmers to bring more land under cultivation.

THEREFORE it is further agreed between the American Mennonite Relief, hereinafter called the AMR, and the Russian Socialistic Federative Soviet Republic, hereinafter called the Soviet Authorities, that the AMR, in addition to its program of famine relief, as carried on under the contract between the AMR and the Soviet Authorities of October first, 1921, will also extend such assistance toward constructive agricultural relief in those districts where it is operating or may operate, as is within its power, subject to the acceptance and fulfillment of the following conditions:

FIRST That the AMR may bring into Soviet Russia or purchase

there such agriculture implements`, tractors, repairs and parts, seed grains, and other essentials as may be needed to further the work of agriculture in the districts where the AMR may operate.

SECOND That this agricultural relief equipment is to be used by the AMR chiefly to cultivate lands for those who are tractive powers of their own lacking in.

THIRD That the AMR may farm tracts at various suitable places selected by the AMR and the entire returns from these tracts are to be the property of the AMR for use in its relief work. Such lands are guaranteed against parcelling out to any other organization groups or persons during the time the AMR is working them.

FOURTH That the Soviet Authorities will give free inport and free export to all implements, equipment, seed grains, and supplies brought into Russia under this agreement.

FIFTH That the Soviet Authorities will provide free transportation and permit reshipment to any point in Soviet Russia of all implements, equipment, seed grains, and supplies produced, brought into, or purchased in Russia under this agreement.

SIXTH That the Soviet Authorities will furnish free of cost all fuels and oils necessary for the AMR agricultural operations.

SEVENTH That the Soviet Authorities guarantee freedom from requisition, tax or excise of whatever nature to all AMR grain, equipment and supplies.

EIGHTH That all the terms of the original contract between AMR and Russian Socialistic Federative Soviet Republic of October first remain in force.

*   *   *

In June 1922, a shipment of 25 tractors and plows was sent to Russia; a few months later a second shipment was sent. This became an important and well-received aspect of the Russian relief operation.

During this time MCC was working in close affiliation with the American Relief Administration (ARA), which had an agreement with the Russian government permitting U.S.-sponsored feeding programs in Russia. The ARA served as an umbrella for various separate organizations working in Russia.

Reading 9
Letter to Herbert Hoover, Chairman, American Relief
Administration, from Levi Mumaw, MCC Secretary-Treasurer,
April 2, 1923.

MENNONITE CENTRAL COMMITTEE
Scottdale, Pa.

April 2, 1923

Mr. Herbert Hoover, Chairman
American Relief Administration
New York City.

Dear Sir,-
It affords me great pleasure to submit to you a brief
report of the work of the Mennonite Central Committee relative to its activities in Russian relief.
The Mennonite Central Committee was organized July 27,
1920 functioning with and for seven distinct Mennonite Relief
Organizations in America including the cooperation of another
organization in Canada, for the purpose of receiving and forwarding funds and materials for war sufferers in South Russia.
Soon after its organization a unit of three workers was sent
to Constantinople to bring relief to the Russian refugees
there and with the purpose of entering Russia from the Black
Sea. At the call of Russia for assistance to combat the
famine of 1921, immediate steps were taken to answer it. Thru
the efforts of our representative Mr. Alvin J. Miller an
admittance into Russia was secured and on arrival at Moscow
a special agreement was made providing for Famine relief under
the name of American Mennonite Relief in Russia.
At the invitation of your New York office negotiations
were consumated whereby our operations in Russia were made
cooperative with the A. R. A. organization and thru which the
work of our organization was greatly facilitatied. We wish
to express our appreciation for the service rendered to our
program in this way. The territory for which the American
Mennonite Relief had assumed responsibility could not have
been protected without your aid and valuable cooperation.
Our Committee is also indebted to your efficient organization
for the transportation of supplies, executive work in the
home field, etc.
The following is a report of the expenditures and present
resources of our Committee from its date of organization:

A. R. A. Eurelcon Food Purchases	$336,000.00
Refugee work, Transportation of clothing, and other items	162,817.76

Reconstruction Work in Russia	29,719.04
Home Executive Expense	7,020.66
New and Second Hand Clothing	240,265.25
A. R. A. Food and Clothing Remittances to individuals reported to this office	181,890.00
Special Food Shipments and other appropriations	15,000.00
Resources on hand	25,000.00
Grand Total	$997,712.71

It is estimated that at least $100,000.00 more have been contributed by our people for individual food and clothing remittances and other forms of relief, bringing the total expenditures over One Million Dollars.

The highest number of daily rations given at any time were about 35,000. Our present program calls for 20,000 daily rations which must be maintained until the next harvest.

We are also supporting a reconstruction program being carried out under a special agreement with the Russian Soviet Government. Under this special agreement fifty tractors with a two bottom plow for each outfit are being operated under the direction of our personnel. It is hoped that enough land will be brought under cultivation to afford enough food to make the vicinities under the care of our organization self-supporting after the next harvest. Due attention is given to the supplying of live stock and other necessities in agricultural pursuits.

Thanking you again for your valuable assistance in this work and trusting to have your continued cooperation as long as your organization is being maintained in this field, I am

Yours very sincerely

Levi Mumaw
Secretary-Treasurer.

M.

*   *   *

Orie Miller's report to the MCC meeting held at Chicago on December 27, 1922, outlines the work of the MCC's first major project, the Constantinople unit.

Reading 10
The Gospel Herald (XV:41), January 11, 1923.

Since the last meeting our work at Constantinople has been closed. At the Secretary's request I have prepared a brief report of our operations there from Oct., 1920, to July 1, 1922.

FINAL REPORT OF CONSTANTINOPLE UNIT OPERATIONS

Funds and supplies received

Cash from America	$125,766.42
Supplies from America	64,952.49
Cash from Lutheran National Council	6,000.00
Cash and Supplies from Near East Relief	2,638.36
Enns fund from America	300.00
Interest on bank deposits	815.32
Items in exchange	265.97
Total	$200,738.56

Funds and Supplies forwarded to Russia

Cash left with C. Kratz	$ 941.00
Value supplies lost in Wrangle debacle	2,641.20
Supplies taken to Russia by Slagel and cash forwarded to Miller in Russia	41,623.82
Total	$ 48,356.02

Funds and Supplies expended as loans

To 64 Russian refugees for coming to Am. (add for Jno. N. & A. Friesen)	14,462.31
To 18 Russian refugees staying in Constantinople-later to U.S.	2,849.02
To 3 Russian refugees who went to Holland	486.54
To 17 Russian refugees who went to Germany	2,349.97
To 8 Russian refugees who went to Palestine	1,049.41
To Lutherans in Mennonite Home	9,000.00
Total	$ 30,197.25

Funds and Supplies expended in Constantinople

Value of clothing distributed	$ 39,976.91
Cash & Supplies for orphanage	32,008.90
Cash donations to other organizations	3,360.64
Supplies distributed in refugee camps	2,330.64
General relief distribution	2,585.34
Cash & supplies-Girls' Rescue Home	6,919.27
Relief to Mennonite Home not charged	10,602.47
Advanced for aiding Mennonites left in Constantinople	2,632.50
Incidental & Gen'l relief in closing work, equipment, inventories, etc.	394.48
Total	$100,811.33

```
Workers' allowance, equipment and
  travel                                  $  7,865.38
Workers' maintenance & expense              2,847.42
Cables & telegrams                            630.60
Offices, auto & gen. expense                9,146.83
Advanced to personnel rep'd in America        883.73
                             Total       $ 21,373.96
          Total expenditures of
          Constantinople Unit            $200,738.56
```

As can be noted by the foregoing report, the principal items were connected with the following activities:

1. The Orphanage. Opened in special building rented for purpose on December 1, 1920, for Russian refugee children under six years of age. Formally turned over to British Relief Society on June 1, 1922. In operation 18 months. Average number children cared for, 111. Average monthly cost of keeping one child, about $16.00. This work was in charge of Vesta Zook almost from beginning. Our work in this institution helped a great deal in getting the goodwill and co-operation of Government officials and other relief organizations in our other work.

2. Girls' Rescue Home. Opened May 1, 1921, for un-employed Russian refugee women. Home formally closed June 1, 1922. Number of inmates ranged from 40 to 50. Each inmate paid 5 liras per month towards own support. This work from beginning to close in charge of Vinora Weaver. Total cost of conducting Home during 13 months of its existence, $6,919.27.

3. Mennonite Home. Opened on small scale in Nov., 1920, and in Feb., 1921, moved to Jeni Kuey about ten miles outside the city. Its purpose to provide a temporary home for Men-nonite and Lutheran colonists from Russia who found them-selves in the refugee group. All aid to these was figured on a loan basis. Aid given in this way totaled $30,197.25, distributed as per earlier section in report. Of this amount $14,604.23 has been paid back into the Relief treasury from Mennonites who came to America, and special credits have been allowed to extent of $1,932.11. The Lutheran National Council has paid for care of their refugees the sum of $6,000, making the total returns on these a little over $22,000.

During most of the time the number of inmates in the Home ranged from 150 to 200 with the ratio about one-third Lutheran and two-third Mennonites.

A hospital was conducted in connection with the Home. The expenses of this were charged directly to Relief and not to the individuals. Total relief given in this and other ways thru the Home for which no charges were made totaled $10,602.47.

4. Clothing Distribution. The figure charged to this item represents clothing distributed at the rate of 50 cents per half pound. The number of different individuals helped thru this department usually ranged from a thousand to fifteen hundred monthly.

5. The lesser items on the list represent various forms of general relief carried on by the Unit during their stay in Constantinople. The work in the Refugee Camp was very temporary in its nature, altho a large number of individuals were reached and effectively helped during its operation. The same can be said of the cash donated to other Relief organizations. Most of this covered rent on buildings for housing refugees where other organizations took care of the refugees themselves.

Orie O. Miller
Ass't to Sec'y.

* * *

As the work in Russia developed, horizons broadened, and MCC planners began to feel that the organization should take on a more permanent form, for more general work.

Reading 11
The Gospel Herald (XVI:42), January 17, 1924.
Report of Meeting of the Mennonite Central Committee held at Scottdale, Pa., December 28, 1923.

The seventh meeting of the Mennonite Central Committee was held at Scottdale, Pa., Dec. 28, 1923. The meeting was called to order by the Chairman P. C. Hiebert, J. W. Tschetter, proxy for D. M. Hofer, Allen Yoder, M. H. Kratz, D. N. Cloudon, Orie O. Miller, and Levi Mumaw.

The minutes of the last meeting were read and approved.

REPORTS OF OFFICERS
Report of Chairman

Dec. 30, 1923.

It has been my good pleasure to keep in close touch with our work in Russia by means of the duplicate letters which are sent to me by our workers abroad. By this means I have been able to keep informed not only of the reports of the local committees to our representatives, the official reports of our field workers, but also the interchange of views among our workers themselves has been kindly laid open to me. Our field workers, as I can infer from these reports, have no easy tasks. In fact often situations arise which require a very close and careful discernment as

well as sound judgment. As it seems to me the direction of
the work with the tractors and the contemplated disposal of
the same, have been the occasion of most worries. We have
all reason to be thankful for the workers that we have in
the field, as well as reasons to pray for them and provide
for their welfare to the best of our ability.

In the second place it has been my privilege to assist
in the publicity work for the collection of further relief
funds, by reporting at various churches both what I have
myself seen and observed on the field of operations a year
ago, and also what I could learn from time to time from the
reports sent out by our field workers. I have found great
interest in the work wherever I have gone. In fact an
interest that was followed by a good response until last
spring, when the situation suddenly changed and we were permitted to inform our liberal donors thru our Secretary, that
the immediate need was not so great any more as it has been.

As soon as the need in Russia seemed to be getting more
and more under our control, suggestions came from various
angles requesting a continuation of this work of charity even
beyond the work in Russia for which the Mennonite Central
Committee was principally organized. These suggestions have
crystallized into a movement to organize our Relief Machinery
on a more permanent basis and for more general purposes. Upon repeated consultations with various persons of judgment
and influence, I published thru the papers a general call to
our churches and conferences to express their attitude toward
such movement as is well known to you.

In response to this call the following conferences have
reported favorable action indorsing such a movement: Illinois
Central Conference, General Conference Mennonites, Defence-
less Mennonites, Pacific District Conference of the Mennonite
Brethren, and the Southern District Conference of the Mennonite Brethren. Other conferences have not yet taken up the
work, some because their programs were already filled before
this consideration was presented and others because they have
not yet had a session. From several conferences that have
not yet acted favorably, I have the assurance of influential
men that the general sympathy is in favor of the movement.

Upon this information I feel justified in suggesting to
this committee assembled in which are present three officially
appointed representatives for this very purpose, that we take
steps toward working out a tentative plan for the organization,
in order that we may have something tangible to present to
our constituencies when further considerations of this movement are taken under advisement in the various churches or
conferences.

P. C. Hiebert, Chairman.

*   *   *

During the years 1925-27 the relief work in Russia was gradually terminated. It was not until 1929, however, that aid to emigrants began in earnest.

Reading 12
The Gospel Herald (XVII:40), January 15, 1925.

Conducted by Levi Mumaw
For the Gospel Herald.

A meeting of the Mennonite Central Committee was held at Chicago, Ill., Tuesday, Dec. 30, 1924. A report of the meeting is herewith submitted:

Meeting of the Mennonite Central Committee

A meeting of the Mennonite Central Committee was called to meet at 2812 Lincoln Ave., Chicago, Ill., Tuesday, Dec. 30, 1924. The meeting was called to order at 10:30 A.M. by M. H. Kratz, acting chairman of the meeting in the absence of P. C. Hiebert. Bro. Hiebert took charge of the work in the afternoon, having arrived during the noon hour. The following members were present: J. H. Mellinger, Allen Yoder, M. H. Kratz, Orie O. Miller, D. M. Hofer, P. C. Hiebert, and Levi Mumaw. The following visitors were present and were accorded the privileges of the meeting: Eli G. Reist, Allen H. Miller, A. M. Eash, and Howard Yoder. The minutes of the last meeting were read and approved. The minutes of an Executive Committee meeting held June 24-25 were read and approved.

Report of Officers

Chairman's Report--P. C. Hiebert.
Secretary's Report--Levi Mumaw.
Treasurer's Report--Levi Mumaw.
The following action was taken:
1. It was recommended that all funds intended for general relief in Russia and Siberia be sent thru the regular channels of our relief organizations and any amounts intended for individuals in Russia or Siberia be forwarded thru banking institutions or the American Railway Express Company using the channels having been opened for such remittances.
2. That the work and needs of Siberia and Russia be kept before our people and that an effort be made to continue our remittances for the work as the requests reach us. An estimate of the need being about $5,000.00 per month until the next harvest.
3. That Bro. Hofer be commissioned to conclude his

"Letter of Thanks" to the Volost and subcommittees in Russia for the assistance given the work of the A. M. R.

4. That we inform the Mennonite Colonization Board that we will make an effort to supply them with funds for relief in Mexico, if needed, not to exceed $200.00 a month for the next five months in response to a request sent to this meeting. We further recommend that all funds intended for relief for the Mennonite immigrants into Mexico be forwarded thru the regular relief organizations.

5. That the reporting of the Auditing Committee be deferred until such a time as the Executive Committee shall direct.

Adjojurnment.

Levi Mumaw, Secy.

Chairman's Report

Another year of activity on the field of relief work among our unfortunate brethren has passed by. Looking backward, we have all reasons to be thankful for the way in which the Lord in His mercy has blessed our efforts. He has enabled us to again extend a helping hand in His name to those unfortunates; He has preserved and kept the personnel on the field; and also the members of the committee here in the homeland.

Relative to the status of the work abroad and the recommendations that the Executive Committee may have to make, I shall not here speak at length for that will be contained in the secretary-treasurer's report. Suffice it to say that we have again for the sake of unity carried on all official correspondence thru his office. It has been my good pleasure to keep in personal touch with the workers on the field, enough to give me the vital touch which is necessary for a proper understanding of each other. The field workers who have returned report of hard work and many difficulties they had to overcome, but cheerfully acknowledge that they do not regret having undertaken these self-sacrificing obligations. We are certainly glad to know them all well. Those at home and on the way, as well as Bro. Miller, who is still in Moscow.

It has been my good privilege to come in contact with Mennonite groups in various sections of the country and find their continued interest in the work of relief, as well as their concern about the welfare of the brethren in Russia. Quite generally I find an interest in, and a desire for the continuation of relief work even after this emergency in Russia has become a thing of the past. Our people are conscious of the Christian duty of relief for all believers, and they also realize that relief work in time of peace and war is peculiarly befitting a people whose confession of faith includes the doctrine of non-resistance. Since a doctrine that expresses itself positively in the service of humanity is ever more acceptable, and also closer to the teachings of the great Master, than one which shows itself only in a negative form.

Practically all of the larger Mennonite Conferences have taken action in favor of a permanent Mennonite Relief organization, and have also elected or appointed their representative to serve on a central board. We trust that this wish and need of a permanent Relief organization for the Mennonites of America may soon be a realized fact.

Secretary's Report
December 30, 1924

This year has marked the close of our reconstruction work in Russia. The tractors have not been sold but according to our last report received from the Moscow office, there are prospects for the final liquidation in due time.

The field workers, the brethren D. R. Hoeppner, Howard Yoder and Daniel Schroeder--have been withdrawn. Yoder and Schroeder have returned to their homes and Hoeppner has stopped in Germany to resume studies in his profession.

We now have only one American worker in Russia, Alvin J. Miller, in charge of the Moscow office. Each colony or settlement in Russia and Siberia has an appointed committee which has been affiliated with the Moscow office of the American Mennonite Relief. Copies of reports giving the names of each and its Chairman are on file in our office.

The reconstruction work in Russia under the care of our field workers was closed about August 1. General relief work was continued thruout the year in Siberia. No American worker was located there but Bro. Miller spent some time in a personal tour of inspection of the work. Detailed reports of the work are on file for the first seven months of the year. In the July report we have the following:

No. of persons in the district,	32,758
Aid given to those under 14 years of age,	4,502
Aid given to those over 14 years of age,	2,281
Aid given to those in institutions,	165

In this report the amount given for the cost of the feeding per person for the month is 55 cents. Efforts are being made to supply the district with a sufficient number of sheep to provide enough wool to supply the population with homespun cloth for clothing, an item which is sorely needed according to a recent report. The report states that many boys and girls cannot leave their homes because of the lack of clothing and many are being deprived of school privileges. During the year approximately $42,000.00

has been forwarded for the work in Russia proper and Siberia. According to the present prospects, the work must be continued at least until another harvest. The crops this year were nearly a total failure in the Powlodar district.

Certain portions of Russia are again in very sore need of assistance to tide them over the winter months. The Koeppnerthal district is among this list. Funds have been forwarded for this purpose and the need will continue. An early estimate had placed the amount needed at $1,000.00 a month. In this connection we must remember the many widows and orphans who will find their battle for life a very difficult one.

The clothing gathered by our sewing circles during the year has been forwarded to Germany. The need there has been very urgent, and the expense in forwarding to Russia has been prohibitive for any assistance there.

Our further needs will center around the work in Siberia and the assistance that may be needed in the several stricken districts in Russia proper. A very conservative estimate would place the sum of the amount needed per month at $5,000.00 or $6,000.00 per month for the next six months.

Reading 13
MCC statement of intention to aid Russian emigrants coming to Canada.   November 27, 1929.

November 27, 1929.

TO WHOM IT MAY CONCERN:

We, the Executive Committee of the Mennonite Central Committee, in regular session assembled at Philadelphia on this twenty-seventh day of November, 1929, do hereby give the assurance that we will use our best efforts and exert our influence to its fullest extent toward the support of any Mennonite emigrants from Russia who may be admitted into Canada toward the end that they may not become a public charge or a burden on any government which so admits them.

And we further state that we have taken steps to call together a meeting of the leaders and representatives of the different branches of our Church in the United States and of the charitable and relief organizations of said respective branches for the purpose of laying before said meeting the problem of the immediate and future relief of our brethren who are now getting out of Russia or are about to do so, and that we have every reason to expect that this project will meet with the united and wholehearted support of our people throughout the country and that, judging by

the responses that we have had to previous appeals for
similar purposes, we are confident that there will be ample
contributions toward the support and maintenance of any of
our brethren who may be settled in Canada and who might
otherwise be in danger of becoming public charges.

We further take this occasion to express our deep
appreciation for what has been done in the past in the reception of Mennonite immigrants into Canada and its Provinces.

                    EXECUTIVE COMMITTEE OF THE
                    MENNONITE CENTRAL COMMITTEE

              By_____
                              Chairman

                    _____
                              Secretary

*   *   *

The Russian refugee crisis of 1929 called forth a new
surge of MCC activity and helped the Committee to more
clearly define the structure of the organization.

Reading 14
Excerpt, Minutes of MCC Meeting, December 14, 1929.

M. H. Kratz Phila., Pa. presented to the meeting a trans-
lation in english of a cable that had just come from Bro.
Unruh in Germany. The following principal points were given
relative to the present status of the refugees:

"About 6000 are now in Germany, others were deported,
mostly Mennonites. Definite registration will take place
next week. Berlin wishes prompt arrangements for the transportation oversees of these people because of the great need
in Germany."

The other items in the cable referred to immigration
problems and possible solution of this problem. Bro. Kratz
also reported that the German Government as well as all the
general relief organizations in that country have united in
a general appeal for help to take care of the refugees. President Hindenberg having headed the subscription list with a
donation of 200,000 marks. He emphasized the fact that our
people here in America should rise to the occasion and show
by our help in this present need that we appreciate what has
been done for them and we ourselves also bear a goodly portion of the expense involved in keeping them there.

At this point the meeting was thrown open for all who
were present to take part in the discussion in the consideration of the problem of bringing relief to these needy ones.
After consideration of the problem in general, the Chairman
called for specific suggestions from each organization represented. It was found that several of the larger organiza-

tions had taken action and petitions were presented to the
meeting asking that this work of relief be placed in the care
of the Mennonite Central Committee and that they had appointed
representatives to serve on the Committee. After due consideration, the petitions were accepted and a resolution was
passed unanimously asking that the Mennonite Central Committee
assume responsibility for this work. /I.e., MCC assumed all
administrative responsibility for any aid which American Mennonites might give to refugees in Moscow and Germany./

  Upon roll call the following organizations were represented at this meeting:

   Emergency Relief Board - Maxwell H. Kratz, Phila., Pa.
   Men. Br. Church of N. A. - P. B. Hiebert, Hillsboro, Kans.
   Cent. Ill. Conference - M. L. Ramseyer, Bloomington, Ill.
   Mennonite Relief Committee - Levi Mumaw, Scottdale, Pa.
   Krimmer Men. Brethren - D. M. Hofer, Chicago, Ill.
   Eastern Mennonite Board of
    Missions and Charities - John H. Mellinger, Lancaster, Pa.

  A resolution was passed unanimously giving permission
to the Emergency Relief Board to appoint another member to
serve on the Committee.

  It was moved and supported that O. O. Miller be elected
a member of the Mennonite Central Committee. The motion was
carried unanimously.

  The Emergency Relief Board presented the name of C. C.
Wedel, Canton, Kans. to serve as a member of the Committee.

  It was moved and supported that the Mennonite Central
Committee be granted the privilege of adding to it's membership such as should have representation. The motion was
carried.

  The following were elected to serve as an Executive
Committee:

   P. C. Hiebert, Chairman, Hillsboro, Kans.
   Levi Mumaw, Secy-Treas. Scottdale, Pa.
   Maxwell H. Kratz, 1600 Walnut St., Phila., Pa.
   O. O. Miller, Akron, Pa.

Reading 15

Excerpts, Minutes of Executive Committee Meeting, April 26,
1930.

  A special report was brought to the meeting showing the
terrible conditions facing Mennonites in Russia. It had
been learned from reliable sources that at least 15,000 had
been banished from their homes and were at this time objects
of charity wherever they could find shelter. By reports from
Bender and Unruh, it was learned that all possible diplomatic

intervention in Europe had been exhausted and an appeal was
made to find this avenue thru some private channel in America.
In view of these facts and conditions the following resolution was unanimously passed by the visiting brethren in this
meeting:

Resolved.- That we as a group of Mennonites assembled
with the Mennonite Central Committee at Newton, Kans. April
26, 1930 declare ourselves in sympathy with the movement
looking toward getting other Mennonites out of Russia and we
urge that the Mennonite Central Committee continue its efforts
toward bringing these people out of Russia and pledge ourselves to support the movement in every way possible.

The Secretary presented a Memorandum submitted by the
German Government thru the German Vice-Consul of Pittsburgh
relative to the agreement which had been made by Bro. Benj.
Unruh with the German Government for the release of the Mennonites and others at Moscow last November covering a credit
of 6,000,000 Reichmarks for this movement against which credit
such items should be charged to Mennonites of America as may
be determined necessary in this movement. The President and
Secretary-Treasurer were authorized to sign the memorandum
for the Mennonite Central Committee in conjunction with the
Canadian Mennonite Board of Colonization.

3.
Resettlement in Paraguay

In 1929 Joseph Stalin won undisputed control of the
Communist party in Russia. He immediately launched a crash
industrialization and collectivization program. When some
70 Mennonite families received emigration visas in Moscow,
thousands of others rushed to the city in a frantic attempt
to escape what seemed to be imminent destruction. Some 13,000
Mennonites may have come to Moscow, but only 5,671 were able
to leave, most of the rest being shipped into exile in northern Russia.

It was then that MCC undertook the enormous task of
helping those that had escaped, as well as attempting to help
those who remained behind. Neither Germany nor Canada could
receive many immigrants because of the depression. Consequently the majority eventually went to Paraguay and Brazil.
After a sharp debate in the Paraguayen Senate Law 514 was
passed, granting to Mennonites all the privileges and exemptions they had asked for. Brazil did not grant special con-
cessions, but a considerable number settled there anyway,
albeit without the encouragement of MCC. The Dutch Mennonites
provided substantial settlement aid to them, however.

Reading 16
Secretary's Report of Special Meeting, January 25, 1930.

Pursuant to a call issued by the Executive Committee of
the Mennonite Central Committee, a special representative
meeting was held at the Administration building of the Mennonite Board of Missions and Charities, Elkhart, Ind. January
25, 1930 for the purpose of considering ways and means for
the relief of Russian Mennonite refugees in Germany.

Maxwell H. Kratz, Asst. Chairman called the meeting to
order at 10:00 A.M.

The opening prayer was led by D. H. Bender, Hesston, Kans.

The following were present: M. H. Kratz, Phila., Pa;
Henry Garber, Mount Joy, Pa.; S. C. Yoder, Goshen, Ind.;
O. O. Miller, Akron, Pa.; J. W. Wiens, Hillsboro, Kans.;
John C. Mueller, Freeman, S. Dak.; J. W. Tschetter, Chicago,
Ill.; F. S. Ebersole, Goshen, Ind.; Leidy Hunsicker, Blooming
Glen, Pa.; Isaiah G. Ruth, Chalfont, Pa.; D. H. Bender,
Hesston, Kans.; J. M. Sudermann, Newton, Kans.; D. E. Harder,
Freeman, S. Dak.; V. E. Reiff, Elkhart, Ind.; H. S. Bender,
Goshen, Ind.; D. D. Miller, Middlebury, Ind.; D. A. Yoder,

Elkhart, Ind.; Gustav Enns, Goshen, Ind.; Levi Mumaw, Scottdale, Pa.

The Secretary, Levi Mumaw, read the minutes of the
meetings held in Chicago, December 14, 1929 and also the
minutes of the meeting of the Executive Committee held in
Phila., January 18, 1930. The minutes were approved.

The Secretary gave a verbal outline of the purpose for
calling this meeting. At the special meeting in Chicago on
December 14 a special Study Committee was appointed to study
the problem of helping the Mennonite refugees in Germany.
This Committee brought it's report to the Executive Committee held in Phila. January 18 and that meeting decided to
call this special meeting to lay before this body this report for final consideration and action. Since this meeting
was representative of all the cooperating relief organizations and the Mennonite Colonization Board, any action taken
would be considered final.

The Study Committee, consisting of M. H. Kratz, Phila.,
Pa.; H. S. Bender, Goshen, Ind.; and P. C. Hiebert, Hillsboro,
Kans. presented their report in written form and copies were
given to all present. The points were taken up and discussed
as read by H. S. Bender and further explanations were given
by the Committee.

After a careful reading of the report and considerable
discussion pertaining to the issues raised, it was moved and
supported that a committee of three be appointed to make a
more careful study of the report and in concultation with
others whom they may choose to call in, bring a recommendation to the meeting for a final solution to the problems involved. The motion was unaninously carried.

The committee was composed of O. O. Miller, Akron, Pa.;
D. E. Harder, Freeman, S. Dak.; John C. Mueller, Freeman,
S. Dak.

After a two hour intermission for dinner and the work
of this committee, the meeting was again called to order.

The committee presented to the meeting the following
resolution received from the Executive Committee of the
Mennonite Colonization Board:

"Whereas, a crisis has arisen in finding locations for
the settlement of a large number of Mennonites from Russia
now refugees in Germany and,

Whereas, it is highly necessary that immediate steps be
taken to move these brethren at once and

Whereas, we consider the Mennonite Central Committee as
being in favorable position to most efficiently handle this
matter, therefore

Be it Resolved: That we, the Executive Committee of
the Mennonite Colonization Board recommend that the Mennonite
Central Committee take this work in hand. We favor Paraguay

as a suitable place for settlement. We hereby pledge our support and cooperation in this important movement."

Supplementing this report, the committee presented a number of suggestions that might be helpful to the Mennonite Central Committee in taking up this work.

After due consideration, on motion and a unanimous support it was decided to ask the Mennonite Central Committee to undertake the settling of 100 families now in Germany, in Paraguay according to the recommendations of the study committee and that a copy of their report should be preserved in the files of the Committee as a part of the report of this meeting.

In view of this action, the members of the Central Committee present were asked to give expression as to their willingness to take up this work. A majority of the Executive Committee were present and responded in person expressing their willingness to accept the task. Communications were presented from several members of the Committee who could not be present, giving assurance of their willingness to cooperate in this work. The representatives of the different groups and organizations were asked to state whether or not they and their constituency could be expected to have a reasonable share in the work. A unanimous expression was given that our people in general would support heartily this movement.

It was moved and supported that we adjourn. The motion was carried unanimously.

Closing prayer by D. D. Miller, Middlebury, Ind.

Levi Mumaw, Secretary.

*   *   *

In March 1930, sixty-one families left Germany for Paraguay under the sponsorship of MCC. MCC now faced the new responsibility of supporting, from a great distance, the fledgling colony as it struggled to survive in a strange, new land. However, very significant help and encouragement was given to the settlers by the Mennonites in Menno Colony, who had already spent nearly a decade in the Chaco. The Corporacion Paraguaya referred to in the following reading was a New York based corporation organized in the early 1920's to handle the land purchases of the Mennonites in Paraguay. MCC purchased the corporation in 1937, and its assets were liquidated in 1952.

Reading 17
Excerpts, Minutes of Executive Committee Meeting, May 24, 1930.

It was moved and supported that we accept the report of

H. S. Bender recommending the appointment of Johann Funk as leader of the Mennonite Colony in Paraguay...

In view of the fact that the German Government is holding American Mennonites responsible for the credit given to the refugees going to Paraguay from Germany and since this credit is included in the agreement of the refugees with the Corporacion Paraguaya on parity with the funds provided for maintenance and equipment it was decided to ask Bro. Kratz to communicate with Mr. Norman /an official of the CP/ relative to the need of drawing up a contract between the Corporacion Paraguaya and the Mennonite Central Committee covering these points.

After due consideration to the appeal from Bender /see letter following/ for permission to send a fourth transport to Paraguay, it was decided that in view of the favorable consideration given to it by Mr. Norman and his personal assurance of full support of the work if needed, to authorize the sending of this group...

*   *   *

Harold S. Bender of Goshen College, served as MCC commissioner in Germany in 1930 in behalf of the refugees from Russia, and participated in the second Mennonite World Conference, August 31-September 3, in Danzig. The Conference was given almost entirely to consideration of the plight of the Mennonites in Russia. Unruh, to whom reference is made in the letter, was a young Mennonite scholar from Russia who had emigrated to Karlsruhe and became of considerable assistance to the cause of the Russian Mennonites at that time.

Reading 18
Excerpts.

Heidelberg, Pension Cronmüller
June 5, 1930

Levi Mumaw, Secretary
Mennonite Central Committee, Scottdale, Pa.

Dear Brother Mumaw:

I was very glad to receive your letter of May 26th reporting the sense of the Executive Committee in regard to various points in my report II and the cable you received regarding the proposed appeal to Russia. A letter of this sort is so much more satisfactory than the necessary brief cables, that each one is doubly welcome. I wish to reply to your letter at this time, reserving a detailed report for a later time.

2. Re Contract with Corporacion Paraguaya.

I am glad to learn that the Committee is working out a general agreement with the Corporacion Paraguaya. I hope this will be in the form of a legally binding documant, especially if the Corporacion Paraguaya is considering transferring its option to another Corporacion, as your confidential statement about Mr. Norman's proposed visit to Germany might indicate. My chief objection to the harshness of the contract lay in the fact that it prevented our Mennonite Central Committee from protecting in any way its protegees in case of unforeseen and unexpected crop failures or difficulties of another sort which would slow up the full payment of the indebtedness beyond ten years in spite of the best efforts of the colonists. I think a strict contract with a definite time limit is essential, if for no other reason than to make it possible to deal in a disciplinary fashion with those few, the minority, who will be found in any such group (even Mennonites) who do not conform to expectations.

4. The possibility of further emigration from Russia.

We realize fully the difficulties of financing any considerable emigration from Russia, and appreciate the emphasis on the warning of the Committee in this regard. We shall maintain sobriety on this point. At least we shall submit the problem to the Mennonites at home and abroad, without any committments whatsoever, in case any further emigration becomes possible. We have reasons to believe that we could finance the stay in Germany and transportation to Paraguay and Canada, also the purchase of equipment in Germany, provided the reception and support in Paraguay could be taken care of in America. I shall not detail our conferences and plans on this point until later.

Furthermore, we have never been very optimistic about the possibility of moving the Soviet authorities to permit any emigration and are less so now. We do feel however that we could not answer to God and our brethren for our stewardship in this matter if we should not use every effort to aid those in need. A relief work in Russia is practically out of the question.

We (Unruh and Bender) have always insisted that the wisest policy from every viewpoint is for our brethren to hold out in Russia as long as humanly possible: hence our proposal, (if you will examine our report you will observe this) had to do only with those who had been deported or in prison, that is, those who had been deprived of all material means of subsistance and faced almost certain death.

In the meantime, the majority of those for whom we have been appealing have certainly perished. Reports from the deportation camps in the North indicate that the children and others have been dying 'like flies' and that the mortality rate of the deportees has been so fearful that official commissions of investigation have been sent from Moscow to attempt to set matters right. Another report states that the official commission of investigation sent to Slawgorod in Siberia found conditions so horrible that action is to be taken at once to remedy matters.

The same report indicated the possibility that permission would be granted this section to emigrate. If this is really true, we feel like being frightened at the prospect of having to turn down the offer of the authorities to recieve these refugees. It must be remembered that these reports come to us from private letters from Mennonites, and need to be confirmed-which is almost impossible. As soon as confirmation or further information comes we shall report.

To date we have not forwarded our appeal to Moscow, since we wish to have a clear conception of what we ought to do and what is the wisest procedure under the circumstances. We did have a meeting with representatives from Holland last week in Duesseldorf, and find that they are prepared to cooperate with us in the appeal, in sending a representative to Moscow, and in the following relief.

Our plan at present is to suggest an interview with a view to making possible the release of small groups of a few families at a time, since we doubt that the proposal to permit large numbers to emigrate would evoke anything but serious opposition and make any action altogether impossible.

We met with McMaster in Berlin last week, and will report on this conference at an early date, in report III. We have found a way through him to aid the Mennonite political prisoners in Moscow and have deposited 1,000 marks there of our relief money believing that this would meet the approval of the committee.

5. Further movement to Paraguay.

The new permits for several hundred to enter Manitoba have again upset the situation in the camps, but we expect this to clear this week, and will then be able to have a clearer view of the situation, particularly as to whether a fifth group for Paraguay will be necessary. I believe I can secure an additional grant from the "Brüder in Not" sufficient to cover the purchase of equipment for the fifth group, and also a grant from the German government, since every group going to Paraguay lightens the load of the government in Brazil. However, I do not wish to make more definite statements on this until a later date. We feel however, that the colony in Paraguay should be as large as possible in order to guarantee a healthy cultural as well as economic growth. Viewed from the point of view of general colonization politics, a small isolated German Mennonite

island in a great sea of backward spanish culture, far from
markets, is a very weak situation, and one that probably
would mean the ultimate decay of the colony. From this
point of view, the arrival of the new colonists is the salvation of the "Old colony" as well. We regret to learn of
the difficulty of securing stock and trust it may speedily
be overcome.
    6. As to further aid from philanthropists in the U.S.A.
in case of further large movement from Russia, we recognize
fully what Mr. Norman attempted with Rockefeller, but we believe that a direct appeal from our church, backed by capi-
talists of the type of Norman, after the definite possibilities
of rescuing and moving large numbers from Russia had been
determined would still have some possibility of success.
    7. I shall be very glad to welcome Mr. Norman in case
he comes to Germany, and wish you would convey my regards to
him in connection with this matter.
    A detailed report III will follow.

H. S. Bender

Reading 19
Excerpts, Minutes of MCC Executive Committee Meeting,
August 2, 1930.

    The problem of bringing relief to the Mennonites in
Russia was considered. Bericht No. XV by Bro. Unruh was
brought to the attention of the meeting. The situation in
general showed no change and very little hope was given
for any new development in the near future. It was pointed
out by Bro. Unruh that letters from Russia were asking for
a definite answer whether or not it will be possible to
bring them relief. If not, they considered their hopes
were lost and would prepare for the grim reaper Death.
    The Secretary was instructed to reply: We are earnestly
seeking a way to help but as yet the way has not been opened.
We know this to be the attitude of all our people whom we
represent. We continue to pray that Providence may show us
His will in this great need.
    It was moved and supported that we send a letter of
greeting and of sympathy to the World Relief Conference to
be held at Danzig Aug. 31-Sept. 3 stating that we are in
sympathy with the work that calls them together and express
our regrets that we cannot send a representative from one
of the members of the Mennonite Central Committee. In view
of the fact that we have a representative in Germany at the
present time - Bro. H. S. Bender, we are requesting him to
be in attandance at the meeting and to bring us a report of
the work and spirit of the Conference on his return to America.

Excerpts, Report of a special relief meeting held at Newton,
Kansas, October 13, 1930. David Toews was chairman of the
Mennonite Board of Colonization, Rosthern, Saskatchewan.
Harbin was the city in which some Mennonites, who had es-
caped from Russia to China, found refuge.

Reading 20
    H. S. Bender, who had been in Germany and recently re-
turned, was asked to give a report of his work and to state
the further needs as he sees them. He stated that he was
very glad to have had a part in the work and wished to acknowledge a very close cooperation by the German Government
officials, the German and Dutch relief organizations, the
German Implement dealers, the ship companies and all who had
a part in assisting him especially Bro. B. H. Unruh who had
done so much for the refugees. Without this assistance, the
work would have been impossible. He emphasized the fact that
the refugees were permitted to decide for themselves as to
which country they wish to be taken. Those wishing to go to
Canada and Brazil were obliged to pass a rigid medical exami-
nation, this brought more decisions for Paraguay since no
medical examinations were required. In one case about 20
were returned from Brazil because of not passing medical requirements. In this we see the Providence of God in providing a haven such as Paraguay for the refugees where they
are given also military exemptions. Bro. Bender also reported
on the prospect for the 300 or more who are yet in Germany.
A recent telegram from David Toews gives some encouragement
to the effect that he thinks it possible to have them come
to Canada by February of next year and recommends that they
remain in Germany until that time. He reported on the efforts that are being made at this time to assist further emigration from Russia. It was generally conceded that it would
be useless to make such effort unless finances were available
to help them on to some overseas country. Efforts were
being made along this line in Germany but according to late
information from Brother Unruh, no final solution has been
reached. He reported that requests had come to Germany for
assistance for those at Harbin, China and that about 200
asked to be assisted to Paraguay.
    /The meeting decided/:
    1.   That we accept Bro. Toews suggestion to allow the
300 in Germany to remain for the time being awaiting further
developments in Canada.
    2.   That we recommend to the Executive Committee to
proceed with plans to help about 100 individuals, 20 to 25
families, from Harbin, China to Paraguay and that the Mennonite Central Committee assume this obligation on assurance
from cooperating groups to help and that immediately some

plans and contacts be made to this end.

H. S. Bender reported that action was taken at the World
Mennonite Relief Conference at Danzig suggesting that a certain Sunday be set aside during the fall on which all Mennonite congregations in Europe and America be asked to hold
an offering for the liquidation of the debt of the Mennonite
Board of Colonization contracted by the detention of the immigration to Canada. The meeting took no definite action as
the matter must be decided by each cooperating group for
their respective constituencies.

*   *   *

Life in the Paraguayen Chaco was extremely difficult.
MCC leaders made frequent trips to Paraguay to be of help
as possible. Now and then MCC asked missionaries working
in South America to visit the colonies also. The first of
these was T. K. Hershey, a missionary from the Argentine,
who submitted a lengthy report to MCC.

Reading 21
Excerpts, "Official Report of Investigation..." by T. K.
Hershey, presented to the MCC Executive Committee, March 1931.

OFFICIAL REPORT OF INVESTIGATION
MADE IN THE RUSSIAN COLONY OF THE PARAGUAYAN CHACO

I will now take up the things discussed at our Group
Leader meeting held Tuesday and Wednesday, February 24, 25,
1931, with the following persons present: Pre. Gerhard
Isaac, Pre. Heinrich Friesen, Pre. John Funk, Pre. Nicholas
Siemens, Cornelius Langerman, G. G. Hiebert and myself. I
was asked to act as Chairman of the meeting, and while speaking
only English and Spanish, although understanding much German, it was remarkable how well we got along. The following
are the things discussed and the conclusions reached. My
recommendations will be found on a separate sheet.

1. COOPERATIVE SOCIETY
The idea of forming a Cooperative Society in the Colony
was freely discussed. The suggestion was welcomed and eagerly desired. These people had a similar organization in
Russia, when each member paid a fee of 25 rubles, or about
$12.50 gold. Here they thought it would be well to have
a membership of three from each village to discuss all local
problems, and one of the three be elected to attend all
Society meetings. For the present they would have one Central warehouse, and later, as they would be able from their
savings, establish others in the different villages.

When asked if they have administrators among their

number, they replied that they have. I pointed out to them
a possible danger and a great handicap in this that they do
not have any one in the Colony who can speak and write the
Spanish language fluently. They must deal with the Spanish-
speaking world, and my experience in these South American
countries has taught me that if the unscrupulous non-Christ-
ian business men in both Paraguay and Argentina, notice by
their correspondence that one does not thoroughly understand
Spanish, they will not hesitate to take advantage of him:
There will be a constant touch with the business world, most
of which speak only Spanish.

They seemed to realize this, and thought they might send
two or three of their young men to Asuncion to study the
Spanish language. It would take ten months or a year before
they would be able to handle themselves sufficiently well
in Spanish to cope with the sharks that lay ready to swallow
them alive. They think some purchasing could be done through
a German Society in Asuncion.

They then asked if we did not have a Missionary amongst
us who knows both German and Spanish who might lend his services in getting them started and make this contact with
them and the business men. I let them know that we might
have, but this is something that would have to be taken up
with the Central Committee as well as the Board...

4. LAND TOO EXPENSIVE
The next subject discussed was one suggested by them,
The Price of the Land. Unanimously, they agree that the
price of the land is too high. We spent several hours on
this problem. The following are the reasons that they give.
a. Because it is the highest priced land in Paraguay.
b. Because it is amongst the poorest in Paraguay.
c. Because being so far from the Railroad, it should
be the cheapest.
d. Because living so far from the Railroad and world
markets they must pay the highest price for their food stuff,
and for the same reason get the lowest price for their products. (This argument is a good one)
e. There is not enough pasture for their cattle, however being a dry year, I fear, they were not in a position
to judge. There is much bitter grass which the cattle will
not eat except when young and tender.
f. Little and poor water. Some villages have to
haul water from other villages. It is very difficult to
find soft water in the Chaco. They dug many wells that they
have abandoned because the water was too salty.

Mr. Casado recently had a well driller from Buenos
Aires to bore wells on his ranches in the Chaco. They went
down as much as 250 meters (over 750 ft.), but always finding

salty water. He plans to go even deeper to see whether soft
water cannot be found. The water problem in the Russian
Colony is a serious one...

To my question, "What do you think you should pay for
the land?" their answer was: Being so far away from the
Railroad, it ought to be much cheaper than where there is
more clear land and only about half the distance to the Railroad. (By this they meant the McRoberts land)

Since Government land elsewhere in Paraguay is offered
free, they think they should not have to pay more than two
dollars per acre. Some thought it should not be $2 per
acre but so much per hectare (2½ A.). They even begged me
to write asking that they might be removed to Concepcion,
where Pre. Isaac and Langerman (a committee appointed by
them) say Government land can be secured gratis. Both Bro.
Hiebert and I tried to impress them with the idea that if
the Central Committee should grant this request it would involve a great expense so that help could not be given to
their friends in Russia to bring them over, which they so
much desire.

They seemed to see the reasonableness of this, and one,
disgusted with conditions, finally said, "I am reminded of
the rich man in the place of torment, if we can't get out
of here, then we pray the Central Committee that they see
to it that not our 5, but thousands of brethren should not
come where we are, but should be taken to the land in and
around Horqueta, 40 kilometers west of Concepcion." This
made us all laugh but it expressed the feelings of some...

7. THE FAVORABLE THINGS IN THE CHACO

To my question, What are the favorable things in the
Chaco? they said,

a. Doubtless they would be less disturbed and freer
to live the colony life in the Chaco. As they put it, "We
would be less embarrassed on this side of the river on the
part of the Government and public in general.

b. They think that at the present price, that they will
never in their lifetime be able to pay off the land, but
that their children might be able to make a living.

c. If they had been placed only 50 Kl instead of 120
from the Railroad and would have had better roads; if the
Corporation would have taken more interest in them; and
if the blow from the cattle deal, sickness and dry weather
had not been so severe, <u>perhaps</u> they would look at things
differently. This I can well believe, and I might add, if
the representative of the Central Committee would look at
things differently and be better impressed, it would look
better to them, too.

Thus the <u>favorable</u> things that they mentioned were <u>few</u>.

13. HELP FOR THE CHURCH LEADERS

There are three groups of religious bodies in the Russian Colony.

1. The Bruedergemiende, or what corresponds to the Mennonite Brethren in Christ /sic He meant Mennonite Brethren/ in the States - immersionists.

2. The Allianz-Gemiende, more like the Alliance. They differ from the Bruedergemiende in that they will accept members who have been baptized by immersion, sprinkling or pouring. They want to be sure, however, that they have been born again.

3. The Kirchliche - anti-immersionists, or like the General Conference Mennonites. These baptize by sprinkling.

The Bruedergemiende will not accept Kirchliche members unless they are re-baptized, while the Allianz will if they are born again.

... The three Church Leaders as well as Heinrich Friesen who has been appointed to look after the widows and orphans in the colony, were in need of a horse each to ride to the different villages. Thinking that perhaps the Argentine Church could purchase them each a horse, I priced Casado's horses on my return to Puerto Casado. I was agreeably surprised when Mr. Casado said he would donate them each a horse. I mentioned that they need horses that can stand long trips. He assured me that they would get good horses, Naturally, he said, not the best he has, but they will be horses that will last a long time. Doubtless, they have them by now.

*   *   *

The problems of land and finances in the Fernheim Colony became extremely acute. Orie O. Miller, during a trip to Paraguay in early 1937, was able to make a more equitable arrangement with the dissatisfied settlers.

Reading 22

Excerpts, Report of Trip of Investigation to the Fernheim Colony in Paraguay, by Orie O. Miller, December-January, 1936-37.

REPORT OF TRIP OF INVESTIGATION TO THE FERNHEIM COLONY IN PARAGUAY

By Orie O. Miller, December-January, 1936-37

The first and main purpose of the present trip to Paraguay had to do with the matter of acquiring the land on which Fernheim is located. Suitability of location, quality of soil, adequacy of rainfall, relative proportion of open and bush land, price, etc. have all been moot questions from

the beginning. As early as 1933 Fernheim had insisted that
an other visit by an M.C.C. representative was essential
before the matter could be settled. All correspondence since
in this matter proved fruitless. The suggestion to the M.C.C.
from the Robinette Estate interests that an offer be made
on their 65% interest in Corp. Par. and the subsequent option
by them to us finally occasioned the trip in the conviction
that this might lead to the solution of this troublesome
problem.

My own convictions were that is:-

1. We found Fernheim agreed after 6 years of experience,
that the present Chaco location was possible for permanent
settlement and desirous to have it available as such.

2. A plan of paying for the land over a period not to
exceed 15 years, could be worked out between the M.C.C. representative and Fernheim.

3. And the Para. Gov. puts no difficulty in the way of
transferring such funds that the M.C.C. should do everything
at home possible to exercise the option or to secure the
property for the Colony.

. . . .

The first evening Conference with Obershulz Siemens
made clear that a sizeable group had apparently lost all hope
of a future at Fernheim, had therefore no more interest in
land price possibilities, and had stayed this long only because of an M.C.C. representative coming, and for his help
in untangling colony, church and debt relationships so that
their leaving might be as brethren and peaceful.

In this connection Siemens mentioned the original group
debt responsibility as fraught in the present circumstances
with much trouble. He also suggested M.C.C. encouragement
to a beginning of debt repayment by allowing cattle and
oxen repayments in kind...

. . . .

Conclusions

1. In a group of 430 families--even Mennonite families--
gathered as these were, there are bound to be some drones,
some rolling stones, some proverbial misfits or some who
are soon at cross purposes with recognized authority. The
necessary strict discipline--particularly of the past two
years--which however was probably the only resource that
saved many from real hunger--irkes others. Continued drouth,
limited diet, grasshoppers plague slowly sapped the hope of
many more. However, the Fernheim location is in my mind a
minor factor in the present division. A similar situation
would have been bound to come, had the original location
been anywhere also in Paraguay.

2. The staying group of 200 families, particularly the
original 92 included far out of proportion those who have

evidenced the soundest sense in the handling of their personal affairs--and as well those who have church interest
closest at heart. Siemen's made this statement. Comments
from individuals from both groups to be confirmed same.

3. Those who signed to stay, and asked the M.C.C. to
get the land for them did so with the full knowledge of the
implications of such land purchase and I feel entered into
the arrangement fully cognizant of what this may cost them
in future difficult years. In short, I would feel to accept
at face value, their promise to perform.

4. Their experience has confirmed what now seems to
me to have been a major error in original M.C.C. Corp. Para.
thinking in regard to Chaco land climate--market possibilities.
100 acres...is not sufficient in the Chaco to take a family
thru for same reasons as would obtain in Western Kansas,
Canada or anywhere else with like soil, rainfall and marketing
conditions. The decision of the 200 families to spread over
20,000 hectares is a logical move to correct this error.
Development of the cattle industry, rebuilding the soil thru
rest periods legume grasses are not possibilities.

*   *   *

During World War II, additional problems arose in the
colonies.

Reading 23
Excerpt, Minutes of Executive Committee Meeting, April 13, 1940.

The chairman reported information received concerning
the development of disturbing nationalistic trends in Fernheim Colony. It was agreed that a statement of position and
appeal on this question, including non-resistance and other
related matters, be sent to Fernheim Colony and K.F.K.
/Committee for Church Affairs/ in the name of the M.C.C. The
statement will be signed by all members of the Committee.

*   *   *

Later that year, S. C. Yoder visited the Chaco to discuss this and other developments with the settlers.

Reading 24
Excerpts, Report of S. C. Yoder to the Mennonite Central
Committee--Account of Trip to the Mennonites in the Chaco,
1940. Presented to Executive Committee Meeting, October 4,
1940.

In accordance with arrangements made with the Mennonite
Central Committee through its Executive Committee and its representative, O. O. Miller, I spent a week, August 3 to

August 11 in the Fernheim Colony of the Chaco of Paraguay
visiting some of the villages, preaching in the churches,
and meeting with the officials and other groups as the opportunity presented itself and as time was available. I found
conditions fair. The cotton crop was good but on account
of rain it was not all harvested. The epidemic of malaria
had subsided and the general health condition was good. The
morale of the colony as a whole was satisfactory though there
were some who were much discouraged and others wanted to leave
as will be noted hereinafter. For the most part I found they
had confidence in the Mennonite Central Committee and looked
to it for guidance, counsel and help. This made it easy to
work with them and I hope the results of the visit will
justify the effort and expense that was put forth to make
the trip...

The next matter that came up was the disturbed and unsettled condition of the colony. I found many of the people
much agitated and bewildered. First of all I discussed the
situation with Brother Jacob Siemens. He is very cautious
in his statements but I felt that he understood conditions
fairly well. From his discussion I learned that he evaluated
the situation as follows:

1. There is considerable group that wants to return to
Germany if possible and about 200 have signed a petition or
rather an application to do so. Some of these however may
not want to leave the Chaco when the time comes.
2. He also thought that the plans of the German government for the repatriation of its people was not nearly as
definite as many of the people think and that when conditions
under which they can be taken back finally be made known, many
who now think they want to go will not go after all.
3. He said that upon his return from Germany Kliewer
said that the time was not here for the colonists to pay debts.
Their standard of living, he held, is far below that of what
it should be for a German. He thought they should first
build up comfortable homes and provide for an easier way of
and afterwards pay their debts. In this matter Siemens and
the colony officials withstood him and after their explanation of the situation he agreed with them and has ceased to
agitate this point. However, there are still some people
who say that Kliewer continues this agitation. This I was
assured, is not the case.
4. The M.C.C. letter was received and read at a mass
meeting of the colony. This letter has not settled the
situation entirely but it has served to quiet the agitation
somewhat and on the whole the leaders feel that it accomplished
a good purpose. Many of the people had been waiting for just
such a message from the M.C.C. and to them it was a great en-

couragement and help. At this meeting it was agreed that
all agitation should cease. The officials felt that this
agreement was complied with by most of the people...
    I also had the opportunity of discussing the situation
with Nickolai Siemens, Giesbrecht and Epp. These men belong
to the large group that wants to stay in the Chaco. They
feel however that the "return to Germany" movement is still
being agitated. It is this group of loyal people that are
much concerned and disturbed. No doubt some of the rumors
and reports current among them about Kleiwer and his work
are founded on wrong interpretations or misunderstanding of
remarks he has made. The above three men however are responsible and conscientious and I feel their word can be
relied upon. They say that Kleiwer is at the head of the
pro-Nazi movement and is in close touch with the German Bund
in Assuncion--perhaps a member. They say that he is not so
active in his agitations as he once was but that in spirit
he has not changed...
    I felt that what was needed was assurance that the M.C.C.
will stand by those who remain in the Chaco. They have been
our concern and should continue to be, but as to their questions
many are premature and cannot be answered now. I urged them
not to worry about these matters when no one knows what the
outcome of the war in Europe will be nor whether it will be
possible for anyone to return to Germany. I reminded them
that perhaps when people learn where Germany will settle
them or the conditions under which they can be moved there
will be no desire on the part of anyone to go. All these
questions, I assured them, will receive consideration when
the time comes.
    As a result of /many/ interviews I concluded that the
difficulty in the colony was due to the following causes:

    1. Unruh's evident pro-Nazism and his encouragement
for the colonists to return to Germany or to German posses-
sions. They have great confidence in this man and a word
spoken against him will not soon be forgotten.
    2. Kliewer's pro-Nazi agitation. This is very unfor-
tunate. He is one of the most forceful personalities in
the colony. He is friendly, and pleasing in his manners
and has all the qualities it takes to make a useful and influential leader and teacher. They say that before he went
to Germany he was one of the most ardent boosters for the
Chaco they had. After his return he was thoroughly saturated
with the Nazi spirit. He was one of the leaders in circu-
lating the following paper which is an application for German
citizenship and re-patriatism. It was signed by 188 people.
This paper is now in the hands of the German officials in
Assuncion.

Application of Russian-German   Fernheim, 26 of May, 1940
Colonist of the colony Fernheim
for citizenship.

To the German Government Representative in Assuncion:
   We, the undersigned Russian-German settlers, male and
female, of the colony Fernheim in the Chaco ask for acceptance into the German Union of States. Because of our flight
from Russia, we have all lost our former citizenship and now
have lived for more than ten years as people without a country in Paraguay. After 1933 our common interest with the
German people has become ever clearer to us. The ten colo-
nial years and the conditions in this country have persuaded
us that we will never find a homeland here. We see the
greatest dangers here for us and our children for whom we
left Russia. Above all we will not be able to keep up our
cultural heritage.
   After the feeling of national German ties was awakened
in us, we do not wish to face this danger idly, but we wish
to do everything to keep and insure our German type. Since
we are people without a country and therefore have no voice
in government, acceptance in the German Union of States would
be an insurance for us and our posterity. We believe we owe
this to our children and not last also to the German people
to take this step. We are prepared to fit ourselves into
the German National State, and like every other German citizen do our duty unto the uttermost for the German Fatherland.
We therefore pray once more for consideration of our request
in the light of our situation and that steps be taken toward
our naturalization.

                                    188 signatures

   ...The situation is not hopeless. The people all have
confidence in the M.C.C. and a warm sympathic letter from
the committee with some tangible expression of its confidence and love for the brotherhood in the Chaco will mean
a good deal. If possible some warm hearted minister who can
preach good German, who comes from the Russian Mennonite
group in America, and who knows the North American friends
and relatives of the Fernheimers should spend not less than
two months in the colony within the next year. He should be
free to preach for them and visit them in their homes. He
should have time to discuss with people their personal problems. This in my opinion will be the best kind of help we
can give them. These people have done wonders in the Chaco
and in another 10 years they will reap the fruit of their
hard toil. Unless something unforeseen happens, their
hardest years are past now...
   Bro. Litwiller accompanied me on this trip and I feel

that it was a very good thing. The visit of our missionaries, Shank, Snyder and Litwiler, earlier in the year was unfortunate. They left the Chaco with a one-sided view of the situation and while in the colony took the liberty to express themselves on issues that were delicate for the wisest and best informed. They meant well but it would have been better if they had confined themselves to the preaching of the gospel and left the problems of the day for some one else. Bro. Litwiler confined his talks to the Mission work in the Argentine and as a result he was not involved. Harder requested him to make a statement to the church expressing his regret at what had happened on his former visit and asking the pardon of those whom he may have wronged. This he did very nicely and I think it helped to clear the way for him. He preaches well, speaks German quite readily and his messages were well received everywhere. He made many friends on this trip and I think it was fortunate that he accompanied me...

I trust that the time and energy expended on this mission will prove worthwhile and will result in much good for the brotherhood in Paraguay. I remain

> Very respectfully,
> S. C. Yoder

*   *   *

The following readings give some indication of the mission, medical, and other work programs that began in Paraguay during the 1940's, as well as reflecting the general growth and development of the colonies. Dr. John R. Schmidt, referred to in No. 25, first came to Paraguay in 1941, but returned later and, together with his wife Clara and family, has given his untiring energies to the work with lepers since its inception in 1951. Reading No. 27 shares excerpts from a comprehensive report by H. A. Fast, who was also a member of the MCC Executive Committee. Readings 26 and 28 share the usual optimistic, global perspective with which Orie O. Miller looked upon all problems, including those of the new immigrants to Paraguay from the USSR and from Canada following World War II.

Reading 25
Excerpt, MCC Executive Secretary's Report to MCC Annual Meeting, December 28, 1942.

IV. Paraguay. Dr. John Schmidt's report to this meeting will cover the main developments of the past year in Paraguay. We have noted with much satisfaction the plans and program there as they have worked out and been developed by Brother Vernon and John Schmidt and the contribution of

Dr. Herbert Schmidt, and are happy in the prospect of the two workers, Janzen and Goigley, going forward to that field in January. The Treasurer's Report will indicate that the colonists' debt and land payments were again not sufficient to fully take care of our own fifteen-year Paraguay land purchase debt amortization plan. With this item included as an expenditure to Paraguay during the past year, we have not exceeded the $12,000 budget which had been authorized for the program in Paraguay. As far as we have been able to ascertain from our workers, there have been no needs which came to their attention which relief funds could alleviate for which provision was not made. In the appropriations during the past year, the total of $25.00 for the Chaco road project was included, although the plans for the development for this project are to continue through the coming three years. By the law of average and since the past two years in the Chaco were poor crop years, it may be that the next two or three will have better results. It is our personal feeling that the Committee is now again in process of seeing its faith and hope in this colonization for our brethren confirmed. We feel that in connection with Bro. Janzen's coming service the spiritual life of the colonists will deepen, and ideologies be less confused, and their program of business and economy develop with prospect for more happy Christian community living.

Reading 26
"Observations" by Orie O. Miller in his letter from South America to the MCC Executive Committee, September 1, 1944.

1. All MCC workers seem happy in the service, agreed to the proposed administrative arrangement and want to continue either to conclusion of their term or beyond.

2. The so-called "revolution" in Fernheim was a most unfortunate and regrettable affair. My contacts revealed nothing in the long-time background contributory to this crisis break not already known to the Committee. As to the immediately preceding factors, there is no agreement among those involved. I listened and heard much but have no clearer picture to give than that you already know and felt that no commensurate good could come from further energies to that end.

3. The colony administrative change leaves Fernheim weaker (and indirectly Friesland also) in education and business talent than at any time since the early 30's and accounts for certain emphasis in the "Memo".

4. Practically all the colonists of all four groups are much more settled in mind, and goals, and in their intention to make good homes in Paraguay than at any time heretofore.

5. All signs in Asuncion and throughout the country indicate a rising standard of living and a material prosperity - perhaps even a boom such as this little country has never had before.

6. Paraguay's attitude to Mennonites, her desire for more colonists, the colonist groups' good feeling to MCC, our own U. S. government concerns in promoting the well being of Paraguay, would all confirm the challenge to MCC and her constituent churches now to give of her best in prayer, personnel, and material aid to the kind of program outlined.

Orie O. Miller

Reading 27

Excerpts, Report on Trip to Paraguay, by H. A. Fast.
Presented to Executive Committee Meeting, October 26-27, 1945.

LEPER PROJECT

Discussing the proposed leper service the M.C.C. staff at the Asuncion M.C.C. centre agreed:

1. That a leper service in Paraguay would be very worthy as a thank-you Project and that appropriate steps should be taken by M.C.C. to get it underway.

2. That a Committee of Counsel and Advice in Paraguay be appointed by M.C.C. to aid in planning and in the further functioning of this service. This committee should be composed of the M.C.C. Director in Paraguay, the superintendent of the leper colony, Dr. John Schmidt, Rev. Malcolm Norment of the Disciples Mission, a representative each of the Fernheim and the Friesland colonies.

3. That the M.C.C. get a clearcut final commitment from the Paraguayan Minister of Health assuring M.C.C. of full freedom in administering the programme always with the understanding that the institution would work in harmony with the government program of public health.

4. That with this understanding on these conditions the M.C.C. gratefully accept the government's donation of the land for the leper colony.

5. That we recommend the Concepcion location for the colony but that the exact site be referred for advice to recommendation to the above Committee, final approval being in the hands of M.C.C.

6. That M.C.C. proceed at once with further negotiations with the Minister of Health and Dr. Regier's office in securing the land appropriate and adequate for the leper colony.

7. That M.C.C. proceed at once to select necessary personnel to supervise the setting up of this service. First personnel should include:

(a) a construction director or manager

(b) 4 C.P.S. men with skills in mechanics, carpentry, building construction and agriculture.

8. That the above director of construction as well as the later superintendent of the leper service visit leper colonies in Brazil to learn what they can about the whole plan, life and operation of leper colonies.

9. That the Mennonite colonies in Paraguay be immediately drawn into active participation in the project.

3. Church Building

...If I had known for a fact what I then had heard only as rumor but later found to be true, I would have asked some more very searching and somewhat painful questions. I had heard reports that some of the colony leaders, including preachers, were carrying side arms regularly but since these colonies so often were cursed with gossip I dismissed this rumor as incredible. However, these reports were so persistent that later Willard Smith, Elvin Souder and I took occasion to ask the Oberschultz and the business manager of Friesland about it and they readily admitted it. They said they did not like this practice but saw no other way out in their present environment. In our discussion we tried to drive home to them the complete inconsistency of asking for the Privilegium and for alternate service on the claim that they were non-resistant when their action belied their claim. This conference with these two brethren occurred on Sept. 1st, almost two weeks after the above Friesland ministers conference. We told these two brethren that M.C.C. would be unable to appear before the Paraguayan government to appeal for special privilege for them unless their action indicated unmistakably that they were non-resistant in fact and because of religious conviction and not merely because they were called Mennonites.

Reading 28

Excerpts, Orie Miller's Paraguay Diary June 17-July 4, 1959.
Presented to Executive Committee Meeting, Aug. 29, 1959.

Tuesday, June 23, MCC Filadelfia, Chaco, Paraguay

Yesterday we visited Menno Colony - settled here first and in 1926. We were at the hospital plant for lunch, also attended the 38 pupil Bible Academy, saw the growing industrial center, spent a short time at the Indian Mission station, visited with Bishop Martin Friesen and all had afternoon coffee together in the Dr. Kaetler home. The colony now numbers almost 4,500, has a net annual increase from births of around 3 percent. There are 41 elementary schools. The church has 7 deacons, 19 ministers, 2 elders - and now has 3 Indian Mission stations - with 155 baptized members. Colony

roads have improved so that the bicycle vogue is just beginning. The Colony store has just ordered another 50. These
will call for still better roads. The Indians are following
after in this too. It is most interesting and significant
how these two communities are accepting each other. In this
it is probably significant too, as one colonist mother put
it, that "The Indians are praying more for the Mennonites
than the Mennonites do for the Indians." Both continue to
need our prayer remembrance - and we in U.S. - Canada probably
need theirs too even more.

Tuesday, June 30, Volendam, Friesland.
    This east Paraguay Volendam colony is in difficult cir-
cumstance. Of 2729 immigrants and births - 1300 have emigrated again, mostly to Canada. Eight hundred forty-three
remain, and a good many of these want to leave. Much energy,
sweat, travail and labor plus help from Western Canada and
MCC have gone into this effort. It is still hoped 500 or
more will stay - and it is believed this location and resource warrant and faith in its potential to a living and
community standard equal to the other colonies. Organizing
to more efficient mechanization seems the only promising
course.

Wednesday noon.
    This 22-year-old Friesland colony (906 persons) seems
now to have found its genius and is healthily progressing.
The colony store and hospital and sawmill-industry enter-
prise, and first harvest rice project visited this forenoon
all give evidence of good programming and management and
morale. Rice growing machinery investment of $17,000 ade-
quate for 250 acre annual production, is successfully demonstrating this first year on half this acerage. Corn, rice,
and mandioca plus dairying and chickens for standard rise.
One is glad with and for Friesland.

Saturday, July, Enflight Charter Caaguazu, Asuncion.
    This youngest east Paraguay Mennonite Colony (from Canada
in 1948) is located 125 miles due east of Asuncion - numbers
about 1450 - 250 families. The new international highway
to Iguazu Falls and Brazil bisects the 100,000 acres on which
the two groups (Bergthal and Sommerfeld) live. We left
Asuncion airport at 8 a.m. landed at Pastorio airstrip at 9 -
visited 7 village Bergthal, including central store and saw-
mill and Bishop Falk, and drove 16 miles back to Sommerfeld
for lunch. Then 15 minutes with Bishop Friesen and back to
the airstrip. Colony average family income around $1,000
U.S. - the highest of any Paraguay colony, and almost altogether from lumber, timber and eggs. After the lumber

resource is gone corn, cotton and hogs will develop. The good colony roads - the sturdy wooden houses, the blonde healthy children impressed one. Also after Trans Chaco road completion Caaguazu and Menno will be only a day apart via auto - 3 hours by air. One is also impressed that Paraguay has become home to most of the 13,000 Mennonites now living here.

4.
Helping the "Household of Faith" (Gal. 6:10)

During the early 1940's MCC became increasingly involved with refugees in Europe. It became clear that many
Mennonites from the USSR, as well as Prussia and Poland,
would need to find new homes as D/isplaced/ P/ersons/, as
they were known. In anticipation of this MCC organized the
Mennonite Aid Section in late 1943, expecting that it would
also help state-side in the resettlement of men released
from Civilian Public Service (CPS) following the war. In
1946 MCC also organized Mennonite Resettlement Finance, Inc.
to serve as financial agent for the Mennonite Aid Section.
The two organizations were merged in 1954. The following
reading is an example of the kind of activity carried on
under this umbrella.

Reading 29
Excerpts, Minutes of a special MCC and Aid Section meeting,
October 31, 1946.

8. The Executive Secretary presented in the name of
the Excutive Committee for adoption a resolution authorizing
undertaking the movement of 2,000 displaced Mennonites from
Europe. Moved and unanimously passed to adopt the resolution
as follows and instruct the Executive Committee to proceed:
"WHEREAS approximately 10,000 European Mennonite refugees and displaced peoples look to the North American brotherhood for guidance and assistance for resettlement in new
homes with opportunity for reestablishing church and community
life in line with their and our traditional Christian faith
and practice,
WHEREAS there seems at present no likelihood of any
considerable group being able to migrate either to Canada or
the United States soon,
WHEREAS the Paraguayan government has assured these
groups of entry permits as they come and since the necessary
movement and transit permits otherwise are also assured, as
well as suitable passage, and to enable this movement before
another winter in Europe,
BE IT RESOLVED that the Mennonite Central Committee ap-
prove such initial migration group up to 2,000 souls--this
migration to be facilitated as promptly as can be arranged--
and the several MCC offices and facilities involved charged
with moving forward with this project as economically but

expeditiously as possible and that our several groups be
encouraged to cooperate as may be necessary with financial
support.

    9. The Executive Secretary submitted further recommen-
dations and plans for implementing the above resolution as
adopted in item 8.

I.

    In line with the foregoing resolution and action, your
Executive Committee further recommends that plans be effected
for promptly assembling a total of $400,000.00 to be available
as may be needed to facilitate this movement to Paraguay.

*   *   *

    The scope of responsibility assumed by MCC is further
illustrated by the following letter of instruction from Orie
O. Miller to C. F. Klassen in October of 1946. Klassen had
himself come from the USSR in the 1920's migration, and had
given most of his time to the resettlement and financing of
the more than 20,000 settlers who had come to Canada at that
time. He not only accepted the assignment outlined in this
letter, but continued in refugee work until his sudden death
in Germany in 1954.

Reading 30
Orie O. Miller to C. F. Klassen, October 17, 1946.

October 16, 1946

C. F. Klassen
165 Cathedral Avenue
Winnipeg, Manitoba

Dear Brother Klassen:

    This letter will attempt to outline what the Executive
Committee expects from you on your coming commission to
Europe in reference to the Mennonite refugee group movement
to Paraguay, negotiations for which are now under way.

    I. The Paraguay entry permit as well as the Argentine
transit, as well as suitable arrangements for passage from
either Montevideo or Beunos Aires, seem fully assured. By
the time of your arrival in Europe, the several Paraguayan
and Argentine consulates will likely have full and clear information from their governments. Director Howard Yoder
and the MCC workers who have been serving in the Mennonite
and DP refugee section have begun the processing of Russian
Mennonite refugees fully committed to go into Paraguay. They

have also begun negotiations with the Holland-American steamship lines in reference to a charter steamer that might have
capacity up to almost 2,000 passengers for transporting the
group to either Montevideo or Beunos Aires. No final arrangements or contracts for this charter vessel have, however,
been entered into. We are authorizing you to negotiate for
such charter vessel on the most favorable, possible terms
and for such sailing dates as fits into the group assembling
schedule. You are free to negotiate for up to 2,000 individuals for this sending. You will keep us advised the necessary
on our part to implement the contract for this charter as
soon as you have negotiated.

II. In the matter of who is to be included in this group
to Paraguay and who not, the Committee is leaving that to
your judgment for final decision and with power to act. Correspondence with our workers in Europe have outlined the
Committee's mind in this. As far as at all possible, folks
to be included must themselves be fully and freely committed
to migrating to Paraguay and with as clear an understanding
as possible of all the implications involved in such decision
and also of the Mennonite Central Committee's relationship
to this movement, limitations of its responsibility, a clear
understanding on the immigrants part of his responsibility
to the Committee, to Paraguay, and to the colonist group
there. We are leaving it to your judgment too as to how the
individuals are to be counselled who cannot come to a clear
decision or conclusion themselves. We are also leaving it
to you to represent the MCC mind and attitude to the concerned
powers that be in Europe.

III. From the time of your arrival in Europe you are
also in charge with power to act for the Committee in all
matters having to do with making arrangements for the embarkation of the immigrants and for the trip to Montevideo or
Beunos Aires and for the necessary organization of the immigrants themselves and of MCC worker assistance--this both for
assembling and embarking the passengers and for the trip itself. In regard to MCC workers on the field for whom you
will need to arrange in connection with this task, you will,
of course deal with Director Howard Yoder or his successor.

IV. Our understanding with our Paraguayan colonist
groups and our MCC organization in Paraguay is that up to
1,000 immigrants be distributed there in the following proportions: 500 to Fernheim Colony, 200 to Friesland Colony.
Menno Colony has committed itself to receive about 225 but
stated that they will try to take care of 300. These colonist
groups have given us assurance that they would receive these
totals on debarkation at Rosario and Puerto Casado and provide for the immigrants further in the matter of rehabilitation and settlement without further expense from the MCC.

In the matter of how a total higher than 1,000 will be distributed, we are not yet quite clear. For present purposes,
however, and until you would have instructions otherwise,
one would assume that a larger total would be distributed
among the colonist groups in about the same proportion.
Should this not be possible, the MCC will provide for the
excess in connection with Fernheim Colony. We are leaving
it to you to inform the colonist groups of these plans and
to the extent necessary and advisable are leaving it to you,
to decide at the time of embarkation which ones go to the
several different destinations in Paraguay.

V. The MCC Aid Section and also the Resettlement
Finance, Incorporated, will want certain specific information
in regard to each immigrant going to Paraguay, of which you
will be advised in detail immediately following the November 1
special MCC Aid Section meetings. Resettlement Finance will
be particularly concerned that there be clear understanding
with each immigrant or immigrant family as to the financial
obligations to that organization each one assumes in connection
with the costs of their immigration and settlement. We will
expect you to organize whatever is necessary at the European
end to get the required information fully and to arrange
that each responsible immigrant is fully counselled and makes
his commitment understandingly and in good faith.

VI. We will count on you to keep us advised clearly
and fully of developments in this movement on a day-to-day
basis. The Akron office will arrange with the assistance
of the MCC office in Asuncion for receiving these folks at
either Montevideo or Beunos Aires and for their further care
and distribution from that point.

In connection with your commission to Europe, we are,
of course, also expecting you to represent MCC in its thinking
to all of our refugee and DP folks and groups in counsel and
in relief help that may be necessary and advisable to them
in Europe and to bring to us any suggestions and recommendations
that develop in your thinking as to what steps should be
planned for assistance to those not in this initial Paraguay
movement.

As a member of the MCC Executive Committee, we are interested too, of course, to have you observe all of MCC
activities in Europe as you come in contact with them and
give us your findings and recommendations and our workers
such counsel as you feel they should have.

Very sincerely yours,

OOM:llh   Orie O. Miller
cc: Executive Committee

*   *   *

On February 1, 1947, the Dutch ship <u>Volendam</u> sailed from Bremerhaven, Germany carrying the first group of Mennonite refugees to South America. The 2,303 passengers arrived in Buenos Aires on February 22. Civil war in Paraguay forced the group to stay in a tent camp in Buenos Aires for several months.

Reading 31

Excerpts, Report on trip to South America by P. C. Hiebert and John J. Plenert. Presented to Executive Committee Meeting, May 2, 1947.

Part IX.
The Camp at Buenos Aires

A camp of tents with 1093 refugee inhabitants on the lowlands near the harbor of Buenos Aires. On a sunny day with grounds dry the outlook is quite pleasant to observe children running about, young people playing volley ball and the older folks lounging and visiting or watching the players while small groups usually stand around the daily German paper which is posted at several places in the camp. For meals they march a few blocks to the large immigration dining hall which has been generally placed at the disposal of the camp.

A spirit of unrest and concern prevails because of the long delay in their movement to their destination plus the disturbing rumors of the civil war in Paraguay, in which the local communists fight on the side of the apparently winning insurrectionists. This with the enticements of the large city to keep them in the midst of advanced civilization and good opportunities to earn fanned by Mennonites living in B. A., have led a disturbingly large percent to fear the Chaco and choose to remain in the city if such were possible. Yet the steadying influence of Peter and Frieda Dyck holds them quite well in control while the brethren DeFehr, Schrag and Buhr look after the matters that pertain to the world outside of the camp. Religious services are held every Sunday, and public devotional gatherings quite well attended close each day. About special religious services will be reported in another section of this report...

Resettlement of refugees presents very many unforeseen problems. Only a choice personnel working under the grace of God will be able to cope with the economic, social, moral, and religious difficulties.

In viewing the immigrants there appear traits that must be curbed, actions and attitudes that must be overlooked, yet there is also evidence of much that makes us thank God and rejoice. Valuable Mennonite heritages, as well as evi-

dences of genuine consecrated Christianity are not uncommon
among the refugees.

The women and girls seem to be healthier, stronger,
stronger of character, and more spiritual than the men of
corresponding age. The latter show more marks of the influence
under which they have lived.

The many women who know not whether or not their husbands,
who were taken from them years ago, are still alive present
a burning social problem.

The /Paraguayan/ colonists will need much spiritual
nurture and guidance, to instruct and to motivate them towards higher spiritual planes.

There are among the colonists both at Friesland and in
the Chaco such as evidently are overfed on North American
relief workers who come to tell them what to do. Uninvited
help is automatically studied very critically; consequently
some of our MCC representatives have not measured up to
standard and have become "persona non grata."

For the best interests of all, we should lean towards
the improvement of the quality of the workers even if such
necessitates reducing the number.

The growing Chaco Colony must have further developments
of its appropriate industries for healthy and satisfactory
growth. Provisions which will enable machinery are a vital
need for the future.

The proposed "Thank you" project to Paraguay in the
nature of a leper colony to be established and administered
by the MCC, will likely be impossible of being realized for
the present. Yet, because of its real need and the strong
appeal that it presents to our constituencies, I feel that
we should not drop the matter.

*   *   *

The continuing work in Europe was slow, and often dis-
couraging. Now and then the trickle of emigration was swelled
by the departure of further transports to Paraguay and Uruguay
and, increasingly, to Canada.

Reading 32
Excerpts, Report of William T. Snyder to a special meeting
of MCC and Aid Section, May 3, 1947.

II. EUROPE

Aside from the VOLENDAM group, only a trickle of Mennonite refugees have gone from Europe. We were able to gain
quota admission into the United States for two Russian
Mennonite families of eight individuals who resided in Holland for the past several years. Another Mennonite woman

is now enroute from Berlin to join her son in the United
States. Five Mennonite immigrants have been admitted to
Canada; two other will soon sail from Holland for Canada via
New York. We are hopeful that this small beginning may soon
enlarge to permit others to leave their present difficult
situations in Europe.

VI. THE PRESENT OUTLOOK

As we look toward the future with the developments of
the past several months to guide us, it is evident that our
further task of helping Mennonite refugees to new homelands
looms large. The cost of the movement to Paraguay and the
resettlement needs the colonists face are indicative of the
financial requirements that further migration will entail.
We have reason to hope that intergovernmental assistance
for future movements will be given, but the amount is uncertain and, therefore, cannot be definitely taken into our
plans at this time. We are gratified that the governments
with which we must deal for further refugee migration have
already shown a genuine concern for the Mennonite refugees
and at appropriate times have fully cooperated with our MCC
personnel.

The refugees will not only require our material help
in reaching new homes where better conditions will enable
them to live and worship without molestation, but they will
also require further help in developing strong spiritual
lives and churches. The past years of strife and totalitarianism in Europe have not enabled the present refugees,
particularly the younger folk, to receive the Christian
nurture that otherwise would have been possible. This condition comes to us as perhaps the most challenging and important phase of our rehabilitation and resettlement program for the years ahead.

Reading 33

Excerpts, Report by Siegfried Janzen of work in the Cronau,
Germany, refugee camp. Presented to the Executive Committee
September 20, 1947.

(c) Community life.
The date when the requisitioning of our camp buildings
went into effect was March 25. The buildings were: a large
dance hall, a former club building, a villa. Even after
having strung wires and hung blankets across the half, and
thereby primitively partitioning rooms for families, the
family-life, at its best, is not very private. However, the
people have made the best of it. Camp regulations have been
introduced - and they are being enforced too. Kitchen per-

sonnel has been appointed, cleaning squads assumed their responsibility, laundry days were arranged for, a Kindergarten
as well as a school was started, guards were posted at the
gates, camp nurses started their duties and the whole camp
buzzed with activities. Since then other endeavors have
also been started such as young people's organization, Sunday
schools and choirs. Also, each evening, the large family
gathers for a short period of devotion. Each Sunday they
gather for worship.

Continually we also stress the point that healthy
people must work. We are very happy that our folks cooperate
in this and as of date, nearly all who are not occupied with
camp duties are employed elsewhere in the city. And in addition to that, a group of men and some women leave camp every
morning to work in the peat fields nearby. (Of course a
wise man must prepare to meet the cold spells of winter.)

Another few words regarding the school life. Fortunately,
happy and satisfactory arrangements could be made with the
local school board. Very generously they are allowing our
school to make use of the classrooms in their school building
every afternoon. In this way the problem of obtaining classrooms, tables, chairs, benches, chalk, etc., is automatically
taken care of. The school started with a Kindergarten. It
was very small then. Today it has more than a hundred pupils
and four teachers. The work of the teachers is not easy as
with each week new pupils arrive. And many of the pupils
have missed long periods from school attendance. However,
the teachers are doing a splendid job and we are very happy
that this is possible.

Summing up: The community life of the camp is bearable.
It is much better and stands on a much higher level than any
found in other D. P. camps. Individual family life, however,
suffers.

5. The spiritual need among the refugees, and what has
been done to solve it.

I approach this subject with rather a heavy heart. The
bare fact that these people are refugees, ought to move any-
body to sympathy. Though however great their material need
is, it certainly does not compare with the spiritual. Har-
rowing experiences of the past have hideously seared that
which was sacred. Even during the last quarter century, the
spiritual life in Russia has been crippled and all churches
were closed. Those who cherished the church and held it dear
naturally refused to surrender their faith. Privately and
secretly they would teach their children and try to persuade
them to accept the faith of the fathers. The schools, however, taught the children differently. Communism was clev-
erly imbibed and the child was slowly turned from the sound
doctrinal truths. I am convinced that we who have never ex-

perienced this will never fully be able to comprehend or
understand the situation which invariably and ultimately
was created. One of the refugees sized it up with the following words: "It hurts your inner self, when walking by
the church in which you regularly worshipped, you hear the
oxen in it, as they feed." And then the war came along!

Although camp life does not encourage privacy for
family life, it nevertheless provides a spiritual atmosphere.
Because the MCC witness prevails in the camp, many harmful
influences coming from negative sources are counteracted.
Sunday schools for children, young peoples' endeavors, evening
devotions and the weekly Sunday morning services help to
build a strong Christian spirit within the camp. On the
other hand, however, camp life also present many opposite
possibilities, especially to the young people. The group
is crowded into too close quarters. Not all are occupied
enough. Considering their unbringing, their experiences
during the war and their present environment, one will
readily agree that the group in camps positively ought to
be led by a strong, spiritual-minded man. It must be one
who can win the favor and confidence of the young people.
I firmly believe that one of the Mennonite Central Committee's
concerns should include: providing sound Christian teaching
and care for the refugee camps it opens.

Reading 34
Excerpts, Report of Mennonite Aid Section to special MCC
meeting, July 17, 1949.

I.

The past six months have been marked by important steps
in the movement of the Mennonite refugees in Europe. Approximately 1,618 were taken to South America aboard the two International Refugee Organization controlled vessels and several
hundred were moved to Canada also in conjunction with the
International Refugee Organization. Our difficulties continue,
however, since it requires constant effort to interpret the
unique background of the Mennonite refugees and thereby
maintain their eligibility for inter-governmental migration
assistance. It is apparent that our difficulties in connection
with eligibility, transportation, and screening will not
cease until practically all the Mennonite refugees are out
of Europe.

*   *   *

Initially Canada was slow to accept immigrants, and
entry requirements were very difficult for the refugees to
meet. But by 1953 a large number of European Mennonites had
gained entry.

Reading 35
Report on Canadian Immigration to the Mennonite Central
Committee, by J. J. Thiessen, Chairman of Canadian Mennonite
Board of Colonization, March 22, 1952.

Immigration to Canada is continuing and during the year
of 1951, 1,118 Mennonite immigrants were brought to Canada.
Most of these were Danzig and Prussian Mennonites. Of the
Russian and Polish Mennonite refugees only the hard core
cases remain to be resettled and we are glad that their number
is steadily decreasing since some of the medical and security
rejects have recently come over. We are continuing our
efforts on behalf of the remaining special cases.

The total of Mennonite immigrants that have come to
Canada since 1947 now stands at 7,874:

	From Europe	-	7,518
"	China	-	26
"	Paraguay	-	295
"	Brazil	-	31
"	Uruguay	-	4
	Total		7,874

According to their first destination in Canada the
distribution as to provinces is as follows:

Prince Ed. Island	2
New Brunswick	2
Quebec	7
Ontario	1202
Manitoba	2517
Saskatchewan	1119
Alberta	1053
British Columbia	1972
Total:	7874

Our Mennonite churches in Canada have raised over one
million dollars to make the immigration possible. The Canadian Mennonite Board of Colonization has granted loans to
applicants who were unable to pay the transportation expenses
for their relatives and friends to the extent of $137,611.81.
Over $100,000.00 have already been repaid.

At the present time most of the immigrants are coming
to Canada under the Mennonite Credit Movement. On May 24th,
1951, a new credit agreement was signed between the Canadian
Mennonite Board of Colonization and the Canadian Pacific
Railway Company, under which the transportation company is
extending to us a credit of $180,000.00 for the bringing over
of immigrants. The immigrants are expected to repay their
transportation debts to our Board in two years, the rate of

interest being 3%. Thus far we have used about $77,000.00 of the credit and the immigrants have repaid $2,790.70 on the same.

Our experience is that most of the newcomers are anxious to repay their transportation debts as soon as possible. It is surprising how many of them have not only repaid their debts, but have acquired their own homes. Unfortunately land settlement opportunities at present are scarce for people without capital and this is one of the reasons why so many of the recent immigrants are concentrating in large cities, where better paid employment is available. Many are joining our existing Mennonite churches and taking an active part in church and conference endeavours. There are, however, also exceptions. Some people find it very hard to adjust themselves in Canada. We must keep in mind that the immigrants from Russia have lived under the star of Moscow for over 25 years while we enjoyed religious freedom here. So we have to be patient with them. We consider it very beneficial to have some of the immigrant ministers travel through our provinces and visit the newcomers with whom they have shared so many experiences in Russia and during their displacement in Europe.

In many cases of serious illness, large hospital expenses were incurred by immigrants which they are unable to pay themselves. Our Board in cooperation with the provincial committees have given the necessary financial assistance in meeting the expenses. A number of immigrants also had to be admitted into mental institutions and as a result their deportation was ordered by the immigration authorities. Through the intervention of the Board and the provincial committees, deportation proceedings could be stopped in all cases thus far.

On May 17th it will be 30 years since the Canadian Mennonite Board of Colonization was organized. The Lord has graciously blessed our work and we were able to assist about 21,000 Mennonites in the period of 1923 - 1930 and nearly 8,000 in recent years to come to Canada and to find new homes here. We pray that the Lord may continue to bless our efforts to serve our brethren.

5.
South America Update: Uruguay, Brazil, Mexico

Mennonites first came to Paraguay as settlers from Canada in 1926. When they were finally able to occupy their lands in 1928, they called the settlement Menno Colony. From 1930-32 approximately 2,000 Mennonite refugees from Russia, referred to in Chapter I, settled near the first group in what they called Fernheim Colony. Pioneering was very difficult. In 1937 some 750 members of the Fernheim Colony moved to East Paraguay, and closer to the capitol Asuncion, calling their settlement Friesland. In 1941 about 350 Hutterian Brethren, who had suffered hardships first in Germany and then in England, were helped by the MCC to locate in Paraguay near the Friesland Colony. A brief description of the help given by MCC is recorded by John D. Unruh in the following account.

Reading 36
John D. Unruh, In The Name Of Christ. Scottdale: Herald Press, 1952, Pp. 211, 215.

From the time of Dr. John Schmidt's first entry into the Chaco in 1941 until the close of 1946, the MCC's program in Paraguay had been greatly expanded. By the latter date twenty-five workers were connected with the program. The relief activities consisted of services both to the Mennonites and the native Paraguayans. For the natives, the child-feeding project in Itacurubi and the hookworm project in the same place were fairly successful attempts to express an appreciation for Paraguay's continued open heart to Mennonites. The proposed leper colony was still pending. The aids to the Mennonite colonies were varied. There was the significant medical service at Philadelphia, the experimental farm near by, the road and telephone project, personnel for the Central School, industrial aids such as the cottonseed oil press and refinery, personnel to counsel in economic matters, and the center in Asuncion with its varied functions including ministerial personnel. To these could be added the training of a number of Mennonite young people in American Mennonite colleges.

Early in 1948 the MCC inaugurated a gifts-in-kind program in the United States and Canada. The plan was to collect utensils, tools, and machinery for the new settlers in Paraguay, and later in Uruguay.

The response exceeded all anticipation. At the Executive Committee meeting in April 2, 1949, Orie O. Miller reported that the tools received were "far in excess of expectations and of capacity to warehouse, finances to ship, and personnel to receive in South America." It was agreed to close the gifts-in-kind campaign immediately and to make appeals for funds to pay shipping, crating, and storage costs.

As funds became available these implements were shipped to Paraguay and Uruguay. There they met a real need and appreciative recipients. Some of the larger machines that could not be directly used in connection with the agricultural economy there were utilized in other ways by the village blacksmiths. Homer Martin, MCC worker who aided in the distribution of the tools in Paraguay, felt that "our folks and churches in North America gave as strong a testimony in this manner by these gifts given 'silently, in the name of Christ' as any testimony they could have given."

In addition to the used tools, the MCC purchased and sent to Paraguay six new tractor-plow outfits and several used steam engines.

*   *   *

Following World War II MCC helped to resettle the refugees in Paraguay and Uruguay as mentioned earlier. Neuland Colony, located in the Chaco near Fernheim, was organized in June, 1947 and by 1948 had a population of 2389; Volendam Colony, organized in July, 1947 near Friesland in East Paraguay, had a population of 1723 in 1948. A group of 752 persons from the Danzig and Polish areas of former Mennonite settlements, located in Uruguay in October, 1948, with El Ombu as their colony center. MCC became deeply involved in helping all of these later colonies to become self-supporting.

Reading 37
Memorandum of Understanding between the Mennonite Immigrants in Uruguay (#483) and the MCC. Executive Committee Meeting, July 8, 1950.

Through the wonderful Grace of God it has been possible for the Mennonite Central Committee and its co-workers to open the heretofore closed and unknown doors of beautiful Uruguay to our homeless Mennonite refugees of Europe. For this we are unceasingly and humbly grateful, desiring only that our words and deeds henceforth might also bear witness of our gratitude.

Of the several thousand Mennonite refugees still in Germany and yearning for a future and security, it has been the privilege of 752 Danzig and Polish Mennonite refugees to make up the first group chosen for immigration to Uruguay,

and to set foot on Uruguayan soil on October 22, 1948.
Mingled were the feelings of this group as they turned their
backs upon the crumbled ruins of their homes, and set their
faces towards the new that was to come. In their hearts
was the hope of building new homes and villages again, of re-
gaining the freedoms long lost. But more than that, their
hearts were filled with the hope that they would again be
able to build their communities, reconstruct their churches
upon the foundations of their fathers and to teach their
children obedience to the commandments of God. This latter
purpose also, has been the primary motivation for the help
of our North American brotherhood, which through its organization the M.C.C. stood prepared and is still ready to help,
according to possibility, wherever need may arise, be it in
the program of resettlement, or future immigration, or any
other way towards the furthering of the cause of Jesus Christ
and the building of the Kingdom of God.

In order that this help of the past and the future may
be channeled aright and our joint working relationship clarified it is deemed desirable that a memorandum of understanding
be drawn up specifying on the one hand the privileges and
obligations of the Mennonite immigrants towards the M.C.C.,
and on the other hand the privileges and obligations of the
M.C.C. towards the immigrants. After due consideration,
therefore, and signing, this memorandum will constitute a
general working agreement between the immigrants and the
M.C.C. on all matters pertaining to the rehabilitation and
resettlement of our immigrant brethren,

1.   The Committee, which has already been elected by
the immigrant group consists of representatives from both
Danziger and Polish Mennonite groups, and represents the
entire Uruguay immigrant group #483. This committee constitutes the sole organ through which contact with the M.C.C.
should be established on the part of the immigrants and
likewise the sole organ through which M.C.C. contact is made
with any part of the immigrant group. All M.C.C. help in
whatever form will be channeled through this committee.

2.   Further, this committee shall be responsible for
all assistance rendered through its channels to the immigrant. This shall include responsibility of repayment of
all travel debts, maintenance advances, equipment moneys
and other funds according to specific agreements to be
reached with the M.C.C.

3.   At this time the M.C.C. is in a position and able
to support the purchase of only one project, which according
to majority decision is El Ombu. However, the M.C.C. also
maintains a sympathetic attitude towards projects such as
El Pinar and others, which through their initiative have
relieved the burden of resettlement for the entire group.

4. The M.C.C., with reference to the foregoing article 3, considers El Ombu the settlement most adapted to development of school, church and other facilities of the community. In a special way it considers this the settlement where provision can be made for the care of the widows, the helpless and poor, and such assistance as can be given for these purposes will be in conjunction with the El Ombu program.

5. All families have a right to choose or reject El Ombu as a place for settlement, the committee caring for the division of land and etc. in collaboration with the M.C.C. However, all those desiring to settle on El Ombu must make their intentions known to the committee within the time limit set by them.

6. Within the immigrant group all are responsible for one and one for all. If one part suffers or endures hardships the other part will be expected to help according to their best judgement and possibilities.

7. All contacts with government authorities for purpose of negotiating future immigrant transports are the responsibility of M.C.C., so long as M.C.C. is morally and financially responsible for them, as with the last transport. Individuals coming to Uruguay outside of the M.C.C. sponsored groups are not the responsibility of M.C.C.

8. The M.C.C. Home in Montevideo is first of all the administrative center of all M.C.C. activities, but further it is also an open house to those Mennonites that reside in or pass through Montevideo on business or otherwise, and who desire a homey atmosphere and Christian environment. All expenditures in connection with M.C.C. personnel are the responsibility of the M.C.C. Everyone is heartily welcome at this center.

Reading 38

Excerpts, Orie O. Miller Report and Recommendations to MCC Executive Committee Meeting, March 17, 1951, following a visit to South America.

Dear Executive Committee Brethren:

My understanding of this commission to South America included mainly the following items: (1) initiating Uruguayan government contact towards permission for a second 750 Danziger group entry and formulating procedure for the group's reception and settlement; (2) in light of Director Dyck's May, 1951 terminating service, to determine the nature and form of MCC area organization from then; (3) to study particularly the four MCC Center-Home projects Asuncion, Sao Paulo, Montevideo, and Buenos Aires) towards longer term, total purpose, and facilities to enable same;

and, (4) to review with Brother Dyck and the workers and
colonist leadership the present state and circumstance of
our brotherhood colonist groups, to help MCC determine its
further and longer term program of aid, and assistance.
Other concerns had to do with (a) colonist-MCC debt service,
(b) additional Volendam land purchase, (c) locating and
determining next steps in the Paraguay "thank you" leper
service project, (d) clarifying to those in the field the
B. A. Center concept and determining the administrative lines
to apply, (e) detailing the 1951 budget for the area, and
(f) checking Paraguay and other V. S. service possibilities.

After my own intitial contacts with Brother Arentz in
Rio de Janeiro and a weekend with the Quapps at Sao Paulo,
I was joined by Brother C. J. Dyck at Montevideo, December 11,
and accompanied by him on every bit of the mission until January 25, when he returned to Asuncion from Montevideo after
accompanying the Uruguay government appointee to El Ombu.
Receiving Immigration Director Roviera's favorable reaction
from this appointee's report and the word of his suggested
further procedure, and finally closing the Volendam land
deal in B. A. (with Martin Duerksen accompanying me) were
the only items of significance afterwards... Plans for
our mission were well made and excellently carried through
by Brother Dyck and co-workers. We had possible visits to
Bage, Brazil and Caquazu, Paraguay colonies in mind which
did not materialize and felt no reason this time for visiting
Curitiba and Kraul, Brazil colonies. Otherwise the visit
allowed amply for all MCC interest contacts we felt of concern to this visit. We met and fellowshipped with all MCC
workers in the area, and appreciated their courtesies and
helpfulness to us and can commend without exception their
MCC loyalty and service attitudes. A few general conclusions:

1--A total of from 15 to 25 workers (including wives)
carefully selected and assigned and fully committed, most of
them for 5 year field terms are needed, and will be needed
for another 5-15 year period in this S. A. area,...

2--The Brazil brotherhood seems ripe for academic Bible
school project. MCC should lend every encouragement to an
all-colony, all-group program, and stand ready to assist
financially if and when such evolves.

3--The four MCC Center-Homes should be planned for in-
definite continuance, under MCC direction and management
moving towards self and/or designated support, in character
and ideal symbolizing to all Mennonites and all others our
evangelical Christian faith witness.

4--The leper service project should be developed as
rapidly as possible from designated funds (including such
specially designated by MCC from general funds appropriated)
under MCC administration and sponsorship as already outlined

and in process--MCC overhead to be contributed.

5--MCC should consider and carefully plan sending within the next two years a commissioner or commissioners qualified to study, counsel, and give guidance to the brotherhood in all four countries,

a. on the church's peace position and next steps in formulation and representation of same,

b. on resolving the colony and church educational programs to requirements of the country and its life, and without compromise to church purpose.

We appreciated especially:

1--Noting the good settlement progress in Uruguay, and the expressions of appreciation and happiness from the colonists and their leaders.

2--Noting the changed morale and spirit in Friesland, and the growingly efficient colony organizations there (especially the hospital project).

3--The growing warmness from Menno Colony to MCC and the other colonies.

4--Fernheim's growing to maturity and self-containment in Paraguay, and their vigorous leadership materially, culturally, and in church and mission interests.

5--The many individuals in Neuland and Volendam ministers in church, and laymen in colony organization who in full and joyful commitment are carrying well nigh unbearable burdens through the present severe pioneer testing period.

6--For journeying blessings and God's abundant enabling to us.

19. That 81 km. Barrio Grande farm project purchased for $9000 U.S. open market Guaranies, 150 per hectare, be held available, first to previously approved Paraguay leper project, and second to such other self-liquidating services that may supplement this leper service or other colonist or MCC purposes.

*   *   *

C. A. DeFehr and his wife, from Winnipeg worked particularly with Volendam Colony for several years and made repeated trips there later.

Reading 39
Excerpts, Report of C. A. DeFehr to MCC Executive Committee, June 20, 1952.

As I assume that the brethren from the United States will have reported all that we saw and did together, I would like to express my gratitude and appreciation for the opportunity to have made this trip as a Canadian citizen with my American brethren. With deepest sorrow and regret I note

that one of the members of our group passed away so shortly
after his return. God's ways, however, are just and holy.

I hope that as a result of our trip to the Paraguay
Colonies a number of industries will come into being, whereby these colonies will be able to prosper and improve themselves.

After our group had visited all the colonies, though
briefly, had had many discussions with the representatives
of the Colonies, the brethren from the United States left
Paraguay and returned home. I remained in Paraguay and
spent 2½ weeks in Volendam and two weeks in Neuland. In
the intervening time I was also able to visit the Menno
and Fernheim Colonies. In Volendam my first object was to
become acquainted with all their problems and difficulties,
and then attempt to find ways and means by which they could
be helped.

Before I continue with the situation in the Volendam
Colony, I should like to make mention of a few things about
Friesland. After I had visited the centre of the Colony,
the Cooperative's new building and the beautiful grounds,
the merchandise on display in the store, the hospital and
the new equipment in it, the Central schule (construction
of which is only half completed), and the better developed
industry, I was reminded of the years 1947 - 1948 at which
time there was much strife and disunity, only half of the
citizens shared in the Cooperative, and a group was even
preparing to leave Paraguay. At a meeting of the whole
Colony at that time I was forced to tell them that they
could expect no help from the MCC unless they showed some
unity and became members of the Cooperative.

When I was in Friesland this time I asked the brethren
there how this marked improvement had come about. A leading
brother informed me that they had come to a better understanding and that all have become members of the Cooperative.
Now, all is well! For very many things the Friesland Colony
is indebted to her excellent physician, Dr. Popow. The
Mission to the Paraguayans, of which the Firesland people
speak so much and also write about in the newspapers, is a
good source of income.

To return to the Volendam Colony. In the 2½ weeks that
I was in the Colony I had meetings and discussions with all
the various, existing committees in the Colony and was able
to become better acquainted with their situation and much
was clarified in the discussions. The Lord granted grace
that some could be settled and corrected.

In the 3½ years since my wife and I left the Volendam
Colony much has been done. Most of the villages have good
residences and adjoining buildings. They have fine orchards
in which some of the trees are already bearing ample fruit,

other trees are bearing fruit for the first time this season.
Then there are the wonderful leafy trees, the Pariuser,
which have grown in unbelievable fashion to provide shade
for the homes in three to four years. The plantations of
kafir, corn, sweet potatoes, mandioka, beans, etc. are in
excellent growth, some of which yield two crops a year.

The industry had also shown progress. The recently
established oil press is producing well, and will induce the
people to plant more peanuts. Progress has also been made
in the building of schools, especially the Centralschule,
the hospital, the old folks' home and mental hospital. The
farms are equipped with more and better implements and the
number of horses and cattle has increased.

In spite of all this, all is not well. There exists
in fact an almost depressing atmosphere. There is disunity,
and the leaders lack the confidence of the people. The income of the people here, in comparision to the people of
the Chaco colonies, is but small and many are of the opinion
that the type of farming that they are doing at present will
also give them but small returns in the future...

Then there is the problem of the molestations by the
Paraguayans, against which they receive little or no protection from the Government. The Colony has no telephone exchange. This would not only profit the Colony economically
but would help to protect it against theft and other unexpected attacks. Tehelphones have been received by the Colony
from the MCC.

A number of the members of the Colony wish to leave.
The number who have already been able to emigrate is not
large as yet, however, every family that leaves the Colony,
leaves an unpleasant impression with those remaining. The
greater number of the inhabitants however have, in my opinion,
not given up hope and are seeking means and assistance to
improve the situation. One important aspect that promises
them income is stock raising. After I had attended a number
of meetings and discussions, I came to the conclusion that
the best way to assist the colony would be to help them
purchase the herd of cattle, which is being pastured on their
land, but which is to be sold in the near future. I attempted
to formulate a plan to help them in the purchase of the cattle,
which would also stimulate the interest and enthusiasm of
both the individuals and the Colony as a whole. After the
plan had been formulated, it was presented, discussed and
approved at a meeting of the Colonyamt and the Schulzen of
all the villages. The plan is included in this report.

Before my departure on April 19th a meeting of the entire Colony was called at which I was privileged to speak to
them. I trust that the Lord will give grace that the Colony
might gain clearer insight and understanding, peace of mind;

that the economic situation might improve, and that God will
give them leaders who will have the confidence of the people,
and that all will come to know upon what their peace depends.

The Neuland Colony, The second largest Colony in Paraguay, with a population of 2410 people, has progressed fa-
vourably, though slowly, during the last four years. The
Colony has leaders, who have all these years enjoyed the confidence of the people. The Colony has adequate and compara-
tively good land, a total of 72 Legua. Statistics indicate
that progress economically has been made in all directions.

The crop prospects last year were good, in spite of the
fact that damage by locusts necessitated reseeding about
800 hektars. Later half of the cotton crop was destroyed by
caterpillars. The Colonies were not prepared or equipped to
handle this pest...

Reading 40
Report on MCC Program in Latin America, by Robert Miller,
May 10, 1962.

There are fifty North Americans serving in the Mennonite
Central Committee program in Latin America (not including
the Caribbean). The budget for 1962 is $200,828. The fol-
lowing is a brief summary of the projects:

PARAGUAY

Asuncion Center. This center serves as MCC headquarters,
MTS office, mail center for Mennonites in Paraguay, and hostel for Mennonites when they come to the city. There are
planned activities for the Mennonite community in Asuncion
and recently an auditorium has been added to the facilites.

The Leprosy Mission. This project located eighty-one
kilometers east of Asuncion is a joint medical mission project with the various Mennonite conferences in Paraguay
through which treatment is being given to 500 leprosy patients,
and a program of evangelism is being carried out.

The Experimental Farm. This farm is located just outside of Filadelfia and is a joint project with Fernheim
Colony with the other Chaco colonies joining in the support
of one of the two North American agriculturists. The program involves agricultural experimentation, demonstration,
and extension work.

Hoffnungsheim Mental Hospital. This hospital, located
at Filadelfia, is jointly operated with the five Mennonite
colonies in Paraguay for the treatment of active and chronic
patients.

Trans Chaco Roadway. The main part of this roadway was
completed in 1961. This road represents the co-operative
efforts of MCC and the Chaco colonies together with Paraguay Government, U.S. Government, and ranchers of that area.

Christlicher Dienst. This South America Mennonite voluntary service program is under the leadership of Martin Duerksen and a Paraguay Mennonite committee. Young people are
serving on the Trans Chaco Roadway, at the leprosy mission,
and in institutions in Asuncion.

Chaco Indian Settlement. At the request of the American
Mennonite Brethren Mission, the MCC is assisting in the
settlement of Chaco Indians. An Indian settlement committee
has been organized from which a board has been elected to
administer the program.

Mennonite Economic Development Associates. MCC is a
member of MEDA, and we are working closely together, particularly in the Volendam Colony assistance program where
we are sharing the support of the MEDA representative.

Material Aid. In 1961 MCC shipped $44,929 worth of
clothing, milk powder, medicines, school supplies, and equipment to Paraguay. Some of these shipments were handled for
other Mennonite groups.

URUGUAY

A center is maintained in Montevideo for Mennonite community activities. We are also co-operating in a student
hostel in Montevideo. We are planning to work together with
MEDA and El Ombu and Gartental Colonies in the establishment
of a creamery at Young.

BRAZIL

We are operating a center in Sao Paulo for Mennonite girls
working in the city and which also serves as a meeting place
for the Mennonite congregation there.

ARGENTINA

We are providing Martin Duerksen as pastor for the Mennonite congregation in Buenos Aires.

BOLIVIA

A program of agricultural assistance and medical services
to the Mennonite colonies just outside of Santa Cruz and to
their Bolivian neighbors is being conducted. Four Paxmen
are also serving with the Methodist Mission near Montero in
their agricultural program to other colonies in the area.

PERU

Mechanics are being made available to the Le Tourneau
Foundation land development project at Tournavista, and
teachers are being supplied to the Bethany Missionary
Children's School located at the same place. The present
workers will likely not be replaced because of the Le Tourneau Foundation financial problems.

BRITISH HONDURAS

MCC is operating a center in Belize which provides a
store as retail outlet for the Kleinegemeinde Colony produce
and hostel for colony people coming into town. The store
is rapidly expanding and is doing more than $100,000 annual
business.

A team is also maintained at Orange Walk for relief,
medical services, and agricultural assistance to the Old
Colony settlements at Shipyard and Bluecreek. Two teams of
carpenters were sent to British Honduras last fall to assist
hurricane victims and this effort may be followed up with
a Pax team to help in the construction of New Belize.

MEXICO

In 1961 a team began agricultural extension to the
Mazahua tribe at Atlacomulco near Mexico City. Two Paxmen
also assist in the Heifer Project program in Mexico.

The following are some concerns which we have for the
MCC program in Latin America:

1.   That maintenance of the Trans Chaco Roadway will
receive prompt attention and that we might be able to be of
some assistance in demonstrating how a good maintenance program can be carried out.

2.   That we might co-operate with MEDA and Volendam
Colony members in the best way to solve the economic problem
in that colony.

3.   That the Chaco Indian settlement program might be
planned and carried out in such a way that it will meet the
needs of the Indians and with good long-term relationship
between the Indians and the Mennonites.

4.   That the Latin America voluntary service program
might be further developed and expanded for the benefit of
more young people and a greater service outreach for the
church.

5.   That the Buenos Aires congregation might become
indigenous and related to some Mennonite conference group.

6.   That the Sao Paulo girls' home program might be the
responsibility of the Brazil Mennonites.

7.   That we might know the way to be of most help to the
Old Colony Mennonites in British Honduras.

8.   That we might develop good approach to serve the
needs of non-Mennonites in Latin America and find ways of
working together with Latin American Mennonites in this outreach to their neighbors.

Reading 41

Excerpts, Edgar Stoesz report on MCC Program in Northeastern
Brazil, July, 1972. MCC Executive Committee Meeting, October
24-25, 1972.

MCC's goal in Northeast Brazil is to participate in the process of development of people and indigenous institutions so that they have a greater control over their environment and destiny and so that they achieve freedom, wholeness and human dignity. This goal is accomplished in the following ways:

1. MCC seeks to make its contribution within the context of the evangelical church and to the end that the church will be strengthened and people will find peace with God.

2. MCC seeks to strengthen indigenous institutions and help people become aware of and avail themselves of services available.

3. MCC seeks to work within the context of communities of people and help them collectively to achieve their goal.

4. MCC strives toward an action model which incorporates the lessons of experience but which leaves room for community participation and the unique circumstances which apply to individual communities.

To add clarity to this process, the following alternative approaches are not compatible with MCC program.

1. MCC is not satisfied with a secular emphasis and image. There must be a Christian content and witness.

2. MCC does not create its own institutions, not even institutions which may later be transferred for Brazilian continuation. Institutions must be Brazilian from the outset.

3. MCC is not content to perform services but rather seeks to encourage an indigenous process which will operate independent from and which will continue beyond MCC.

4. MCC is not content to work with individuals excepting as individuals are thereby more able to contribute to a community dynamic. The emphasis is to work with people within the context of community and community institutions.

5. MCC is not content to busy itself with running projects except as projects contribute directly to the overall objective and in which case a plan for MCC withdrawal must be a part of the original design.

6. MCC does not seek to maintain high visibility, preferring instead to have initiative remain with the community and preferring also to make its contribution through others...

MCC has the following strategy to achieve these objectives.

1. The program in Northeast Brazil is basically directed to rural communities within Pernambuco State where desirable patterns of land ownership exist and where people have a desire to participate in the development process.

2. A secondary program emphasis is within the city of Recife. This includes the Evangelical Hospital and other urban programs to be developed.

3. DIACONIA is a good channel through which to work
because it is Brazilian and represents the evangelical church.
MCC has a convenio with DIACONIA which assigns responsibilities
to both parties and which has proven to have reciprocal benefits. MCC program planning is done within the context of
DIACONIA program and seeks to tie in with it and compliment
it wherever possible.

4. MCC employs the self-help, non-directive approach
which seeks to encourage the process of self-determination
(both individuals and institutions) and human dignity. This
means that the plan is based largely on indigenous resources
but minimal budget and material aid are supplied to be used
both within the context of MCC and DIACONIA programs.

5. MCC maintains a headquarters in Recife and MCC employs
a director couple to backstop field workers.

6. MCC seeks to maintain fraternal relationships and
coordinate program with likeminded church, governmental and
private agencies.

7. In terms of size, MCC seeks to maintain a program
of fifteen workers with budget minimally, increasing to 20-25
workers as personnel and budget is available. Also MCC will
continue to supply material aid as available, anticipating
a dollar volume in the range from $250,000 to $300,000
annually.

8. MCC continues to invite the participation of the
Mennonite church in Brazil and is prepared to adjust its
program and strategy to achieve this participation on all
levels practical including program planning, personnel and
funds.

Reading 42

Excerpts, Report on Latin America Trip, by Delton and
Marian Franz. Executive Committee Meeting, September 26-27,
1974.

Peace and Justice

Exposure to the slum barrios on the hill sides rimming
Bogota, the villas of Buenos Aires, the cardboard shacks
of Timbues (Montevideo) and the rural poverty of sugarcane
field worker outside Recife, leaves one overwhelmed with the
inadequateness of the traditional Mennonite concept of bringing a "peace witness."

It becomes very clear that in the face of economic ex-
ploitation and repression experienced by Latin America's
"marginal men" - we must think in terms of peace and justice,
without which there can be little meaning to the concept of
peace. It also becomes clear that in our affluent U.S.
experience, we have not combined these two terms in our thinking.

Could it be that the Catholic Church has something to
teach Mennonites about peace? We have always assumed it was
the other way around. In Latin America there are Catholic
leaders from whom we may have much to learn. After our 1½
hour visit with Dom Helder Camara, I realized that he and
those within the Catholic Church who are committed to both
nonviolence and to justice for the oppressed have much to
say that we should hear.

For Mennonites in the U.S., the justice dimension of
this equation suggests that we must examine more frankly the
impact of U.S. business corporations and the U.S. military
assistance in Latin America that maintain elitist military
regimes in power for the express purpose of protecting U.S.
business investments.

*   *   *

Long before the coming of the World War II Mennonite
refugees to Paraguay, MCC and the Mennonites in Paraguay
were talking of an appropriate "thank you project" to that
land and its people for admitting the Mennonites without
health and other formal requirements. It was finally agreed
that a mission to the many persons suffering from Hansen's
disease (leprosy) would be most fitting, but years went
by before it began. A tract of land donated for this purpose by the government turned out to be settled by too many
families to be relocated. Finally in 1950 a suitable tract
was located some 50 miles from Asuncion at Kilometer 81, at
Itacurubi, and work could begin. Dr. John R. and Clara
Schmidt became the medical directors of the project.

Reading 43
Excerpts, Orie O. Miller May 31, 1951 letter to all MCC
members. MCC Executive Committee Meeting, May 26, 1951.

I. Paraguay Leper Service Project It is about six
years since Dr. Plunkett in Asuncion called our workers
attention to the need of these unfortunates in Paraguay,
and that this disease there was still on the increase and
no adequate facility within the country to deal with it.
Our Mennonite colonies in Paraguay and workers there promptly agreed that service to this need would provide a most
suitable "thank you" project to this country which has had
its doors so wide open to Mennonite immigrants for so long.
American Leprosy Missions in New York soon agreed also to
help in any MCC sponsored project in Paraguay to the extent
of 3/5 of the initial cost of whatever facility needed to
be provided for this service and a similar proportion of the
continuing operations cost. Paraguay Government Health Department has been friendly and helpful in suggesting and

finding a suitable site, and in arranging good governmental
relationships. The other evangelical missions in Paraguay
have also encouraged this move, and are cooperating in ways
that they can.

Only this past January, however, has finally a suitable
site been found and purchased--a farm project approximately
50 miles east of Asuncion with good transportation and
other connection facilities. Dr. John R. Schmidt and wife
Clara who served our Chaco Colony medical needs a number of
years previously are returning with their family to Paraguay
in August to lead out in the establishment and direction of
this leper service project towards the initial building program. A budget of $25,000 has been approved for the current
year and which will be used mostly in assembling and stock
piling materials against next year's building. This current
year's total is in hand except for a further $6,000 needed
in designated contributions from our North American MCC
constitutency by or before next December.

1. If the several groups which each of you represent
would feel to appropriate from $250 to $1000, according to
the size group you represent to this purpose, the total
would easily be brought together, and would leave this need
further to your judgment and the Lord's further leading.
Whatever funds may come to your group treasury or that you
may decide to particularly appropriate to this purpose and
intended for this year's budget should be forwarded to us as
soon as available and before December 1.

Reading 44
August 27, 1951 letter from Cornelius J. Dyck to MCC re use
of deputation receipts for South America Medical Program.
Executive Committee Meeting, September 15, 1951.

As requested and agreed upon I am now, upon completion
of my deputation work, submitting my recommendations for the
allocation of funds donated, and in line with Executive Committee minute 13 of April 28 and May 26 confirmation. Not
nearly all amounts collected at the various meetings are
known to me yet, but with what I have listed, including the
Bluffton churches donation and the Mr. Yoder gift from West
Liberty, we have approximately $14,000 available from US
churches for medical purposes. This does not include the
$2000 given by Manitoba churches now through special effort
of Wm. Enns for the Menno colony hospital, nor does it include the other Canadian donations which are to go for equipment and etc. and on which I will report later. The following
recommendations are based on my knowledge of the hospitals
in Paraguay and their conditions, which I made a special effort to study and analyze prior to my departure, in prepara-

tion for my deputation assignment, and have been brought up
to date through considerable correspondence I have received
from Paraguay since my departure.

    1. <u>Home for the Mentally Ill</u>: The capacity and facili-
ties of the present institutions are very inadequate and
primitive. We have repeatedly discussed with the colonies,
the problems involved. In the Asuncion office we have letters
from all colonies confirming their willingness to work together in a joint project to care for their mentally ill.
It was agreed that if at all possible financially, a new
building should be erected on the outskirts of Filadelfia
and I believe the colony felt it could be directly north of
the present one. Enough land would be included to provide
for adequate work therapy. The project would be directed
by an all-colony representative board of directors and fi-
nanced by all colonies. Because of the uncertainty of funds
available this committee has of course not yet been organized.
Dr. Tavonius is deeply interested in this type of work. I
do not think it possible nor desirable to attempt using the
Paraguayan Asuncion institution for the Mennonite mentally
ill, and I believe this also expresses the colonies' senti-
ments. I therefore recommend the allocation of $5500 for
this project, of which $2000 should remain in Akron to cover
orders for instruments and equipment etc. which will be
placed by the doctors and the committee in due course.

    2. <u>Tuberculosis Sanatorium</u>: There has been considerable
discussion about the necessity of building a TB sanatorium
in the Chaco, but many factors must be taken into consideration. In view of good facilities in Asuncion - altho limited -
and the excellent cooperation we have been receiving from
the authorities in charge, however, I feel we should plan
to continue using these facilities as long as possible since
they are free to the patient and good, and postpone plans for
the building of a TB sanatorium until such time as circumstances and developments dictate.

    3. <u>Medical Literature</u>: Our doctors in Paraguay feel
keenly that they are cut off from developments in the medical
world, which can be overcome by 1) giving them opportunity
to visit Brazil and Argentina occasionally, 2) by having
visiting doctors, i.e. John Schmidt, give them refresher
courses, and 3) by making available to them the current
medical literature and journals from Germany and the USA.
The three chief doctors read English fluently. I therefore
recommend that a fund of $50 be established in Akron and
that the doctors be informed they may order periodicals
against this account in Akron. Three sets will likely need
to be ordered, one for the Chaco doctors, one for Volendam
and one for Friesland.

    4. <u>Volendam Colony</u>: Volendam urgently needs isolation

wards, the plans for which are already completed. Further
their kitchen and pharmacy are totally inadequate and they
plan to improve them. Thirdly, they have a considerable
deficit in their operating budget and therefore need help
in the purchase of medicines and etc. Also they need supplies - sets of teeth - filling material, dental instruments
which dentist Klassen can specify. I therefore recommend
the allocating of $2000 for these purposes, of which $500
should remain in Akron to pay for orders they will place.

    5. Neuland Colony: Neuland has begun building a 25
bed hospital. This will be for emergency, maternity and
usual cases and will in no way attempt to compete or duplicate the Filadelfia hospital efforts. We should in my opinion have Filadelfia remain the central strong medical center
with best surgical and other equipment and have Neuland and
Menno equipped for the above mentioned type of cases. Neuland has some funds for the building but not enough. They
also have an operating deficit and also need considerable
more equipment. I therefore recommend the allocating of
$2000 for these purposes, of which $1000 should remain in
Akron to pay for equipment they need and have specified
1) a box set of eyeglasses to determine what type of glasses
a patient must have, 2) a small power unit for electric
power and light 3hp 11volt AC, 3) a lamp for the operation
and maternity table. It should be a standing lamp which
can be raised and lowered. 4) A typewriter. Other needs
they will specify. They felt that a jeep was a necessity
because it is 50 miles from one end of the colony to the
other and the doctor finds it impossible to carry on his work
adequately, especially hookworm control etc., but since the
Canadian brotherhood will be sending them a truck now I feel
they can use that for the time being for this purpose also.

    6. Friesland Colony: That hospital is operating
rather well of late. It has been a thrill for me to see the
outreach of their service and already that program is probably the greatest mission field we have in Paraguay. Hundreds of Paraguayans are treated there, whether they can pay
or not, they are given Christian love and service and Mr.
Langeman always has spanish Bibles and tracts ready for them.
Their facilities are far too small to take care of the patients
and they must build soon. Also they must have more equipment. I believe this to be one of the finest ways in which
we could invest funds entrusted to us by our churches, and
besides helping the Paraguayans and being an open door for
missions, it is doing more for the Mennonites in colony Friesland than is currently being realized. I therefore recommend
the allocating of $2000 for this purpose, of which $500 should
remain in Akron to pay for orders they will place.

    7. Fernheim Colony: Fernheim remains the center of

medical treatment in the Chaco and help given to that hospital
is therefore also help given to all the other inhabitants
of the Chaco. They are building a kitchen and storeroom and
need help for that. They are planning to build a nurses
home, which they must build to insure stability of their staff
for the future. They need further equipment. They have today a very able doctor and Peter Kethler, their manager is
very dependable and level-headed. I therefore recommend the
allocating of $2000 for this purpose of which $1500 should
remain in Akron to pay for the following: 1) $1000 worth
of tin roofing for the a/m buildings; 2) $350 to be deposited
with Dr. Lohrenz, McPherson, Kansas, who supplies all glasses
for the Paraguayan Mennonites (this would be a fund transfer,
the glasses recipients, if able, would pay in guranies,
which fund would be used for the buildings indicated above.)
3) $150 for a small power unit 3 kw (3hp) 110 volt AC for
their X-Ray machine.

   8. Menno Colony: As indicated, the Manitoba conservative groups have, through the efforts of Wm. Enns, donated
$2000 for hospitals in Menno colony which places that colony
on an equal basis with the others as far as help is concerned.
That money has already been forwarded as you know.

   9. El Ombu Colony, Uruguay: Complete medical facilities
are not necessary there since they are within 30 miles of the
hospital at Young. However, they should definitely have a
first aid and maternity ward, the more so since they do have
a nurse who is able to supervise such a ward. I have discussed with them the placing aside of one room in the main
farmhouse for this purpose. It would save them much money
and trouble and inconvenience. They do not need major equipment, but they do need some instruments, medicines, beds
and etc. I therefore recommend the allocating of $450 for
this purpose, to be made available to them as soon as possible
for the above purpose. They can buy all the equipment etc.,
in Uruguay.

   Conclusions: I have not recommended the use of these
funds to send doctors on short visits to Brazil or Argentina
because Dr. John Schmidt and the periodicals they will now
receive will do much to bring them up to date. The need for
such study trips can more expertly be determined by Dr.
Schmidt after he has been there some time. I have also not
recommended special help to nurses, because they are receiving
help from other sources, such as Mennonite School of Nursing
with it headquarters at La Junta, Colo.

   The various items indicated for purchase have been definitely cleared with the colonies and purchase can be begun
immediately. After acceptance, the colonies should be informed of the amounts they have and against which they can
order. Because of the currency situation in Paraguay, some

colonies may wish to leave all dollars here for order payment
and deposit the equivalent in guaranies in favor of the projects envisioned. This should be in order, but we should
see to it that all funds do eventually reach their destination.
I believe these funds should do much to help our hospitals
and make them more self-supporting, with the exception of
Volendam which will probably be coming with new needs again
next budget year.

Because the churches have given this great amount of
money they are naturally more interested in the medical program now than before. I would hope that these donations
could be made available to the recipient as soon as possible
without complicatons while the gift is still warm, so that
some of the warmth of gratitude on the part of the recipients
may flow back to the donors. Some explanation of their
origin should be given and our Paraguay MCC office should
encourage the colonies to send letters and reports on disposal
and use of these funds, to our church papers in the USA particularly.

*   *   *

An inter-Mennonite Bible School (Seminary) was begun
in Montevideo, Uruguay in 1955 by South American conferences
and the support of the boards of missions of the Mennonite
Church and the General Conference Mennonite Church.

Reading 45
Excerpts, Report of Orie O. Miller to the MCC Executive
Committee, February 24, 1954.

Orie O. Miller reported on developments in regard to
the proposed Montevideo Bible School. (See Minute 27,
April 25, 1953 Executive Committee minutes) In view of
the failure of the original plan for a jointly operated
Bible School, the Mennonite Board of Missions and Charities
(Elkhart) is going ahead with plans to develop a Bible School
under its own management. Nelson Litwiller reports good
results from his trip to the Paraguayan Chaco on behalf of
the school. He indicates intention to start the school in
April, 1955. It is his hope that there can be representatives of other groups on the faculty. There was some further
discussion of the problems related to the establishment of
such a school. H. A. Fast reported that the General Conference Mission Board is deeply interested in the possibilities of such a school, since it will serve all groups in
South America, and is concerned that the planning for any
such school be on a cooperative basis.

*   *   *

The Chaco colonies had long felt the economic disadvantage of isolation from national and world markets. The development of the Chaco highway through a cooperative arrangement between the Paraguayan and USA governments, the Mennonites of Paraguay and MCC, became a valuable economic asset to the colonies.

Reading 46
Excerpts, Training Project for Roads in Chaco, MCC Executive Committee Report, July 16, 1955, item 19.

Moved and passed to adopt the following recommendation submitted by the Mennonite Aid Section but to consider it as a Pax Paraguay project:

Recommended that we confirm the following section of a May 18, 1955, agreement between the Foreign Operations Administration, the Paraguayan Government (Ministry of Public Works and Communications) and the Mennonite Central Committee, whereby the Mennonite Central Committee agrees to perform the following as part of a training project for developing and maintaining low-cost roads in the Chaco region:

"The Mennonite Central Committee (hereinafter referred to as the 'Committee') which shall:

A. Provide a crew of up to seven technicians skilled in the operation, practical use and maintenance of the machinery procured by FOA for, or otherwise made available to, this project and who are skilled in road culvert and bridge construction of the type planned for the Chaco region of Paraguay.

B. Through the aforementioned crew of technicians, provide practical training for selected groups of Paraguayans in the operation and maintenance of road-building equipment as well as training in road culvert and bridge construction, road surfacing techniques and in the proper maintenance thereof.

C. Finance all costs and expenses of the aforementioned crew of technicians including international travel, travel within Paraguay, maintenance and any other allowances the Committee deems necessary during the stay of such technicians in Paraguay.

D. Assume responsibility for the aforementioned crew of technicians when off the project."

*   *   *

The relationship between Indians and Mennonites in the Chaco of Paraguay has been discussed by laymen and scholars in many forms for many years. Thousands of Indians have become baptized church members since the Mennonite immigrants first began working with them in the mid 1930's. The

following comments by Hans E. Epp, a medical doctor who has
been working with the Indians since 1968, provide a good
introduction to the issues.

Reading 47
Indians in the Paraguayan Chaco: A Challenge.   By Hans
E. Epp, M.D., MCC Annual Meeting, January 19-20, 1973.

Background Review
　　Since the arrival of the first Mennonite colonists in
the Paraguayan Chaco in 1927, a good portion of the Mennonite
history has happened there.   It is the history of the colonies
Menno, Fernheim and Neuland.   But they were not completely
isolated.   Closely related ever since has been the history
of the two main Indian tribes in the Chaco, the Lengua and
the Chulupi.
　　The Mennonites did not come to the Chaco because of
the Indians.   They had legally purchased the land and their
biggest desire was to live free, peaceful and according to
the dictates of their conscience.   They were looking for a
new home.
　　But there they met the Indians living in the area.   And
they saw many of their struggles and their problems.   The
Lengua tribe at that time seemed to be dying out.   Mennonites
took this encounter as being by divine providence.   And they
responded to the challenge.   In 1935 an organization, "Licht
den Indianern" (Light to the Indians), was established.   It's
main goals were:
　　1.   Evangelization
　　2.   Education
　　3.   Health
　　4.   Economic self-sufficiency
For the first two decades the emphasis of this mission
work was on evangelization.   Hundreds and thousands of
Indians have accepted Christ as their personal saviour.   It
has made a big difference in their lives.   And it has strongly
influenced their original culture for better or for worse.
However, the new values based on biblical truth have had
a positive influence on the development of the Indian society.
Over the years, the local Indian churches have become increasingly independent.
　　This mission program has been a joint responsibility
of the local Mennonite churches and the MB Mission Board
in Hillsboro, Kansas; and lately also of the GC Mission
Board in Newton, Kansas.   Around 1960 pressure from the
Indians was increasing to own land.   As a consequence an
ambitious settlement program was started.   This was done as
a joint endeavor of the Mennonite colonies and MCC, Akron,
Pennsylvania.

At present the programs of economic development, education and health are managed by an Executive Committee, composed of a chairman and a man in charge of each of these sections. There is also an accountant in the committee, and as of April, 1973, an anthropologist will be part of the team. This Executive Committee is responsible to the Board of Indian Settlement.

Settlement and Economic Development
The stated goal of the settlement program has always been to make the Indians self-sufficient (selbstaendig). In the six settlements today there are about 800 families on their own plot of land. The main cash crop is cotton. But very important are also a variety of food crops for consumption, like beans, peanuts, corn, sorghum, watermelons, some fruits and vegetables.

What have been the results so far?

Many a family has failed on the farm. A roughly estimated 10% of the original settlers have left the farm again and have returned to be day laborers on Mennonite farms or factories. Other families have taken over the abandoned farms. There are some farmers who have done remarkably well. Speaking in general terms, progress has been made. But progress has been slow. And this is what has puzzled many people. Why is it so slow? Will the day ever come when the Indians will truly be economically self-sufficient? These are often asked questions.

Farming in the Chaco is a risky undertaking because of the very capricious rainfall pattern. There are usually several months of the year when there is almost nothing to do on the farm. So there is increasing awareness of the need of diversification of the economy, in order to increase the overall level of income and at the same time cut down on the periodically severe underemployment. Up until now no good answers have been found to this problem. What is needed is a labor-intensive type of industry, because labor is cheap and capital is scarce. At the present time attention is focused on handicrafts and home industry.

Experimental projects with cattle and poultry also have been started. But especially cattle is a capital-intensive industry. There is the problem of leadership. The governing body is elected by the community in each settlement. But Indian leadership is still very weak. Is it possible to train leaders in a multicultural setting? And if, how can it be done? How can the Indian society be induced to take over more responsibility and more initiative in the actual shaping of their future? These are questions that remain to be answered.

Because of these and many other open questions and un-

solved problems, compounded by the very different cultural
background of Mennonites and Indians, a sociologist-anthro-
pologist was called in as consultant. Dr. Cal Redekop from
Goshen, Indiana, spent nine months in 1971-72 on the Indian
settlements to study the situation in order to improve mutual
understanding between the two cultures and to come up with
new and better answers. Cal Redekop gave us some answers.
But anthropology does not have all the answers and solutions,
either.

The question is sometimes raised: "Is the Indian really
capable of developing the necessary skills and knowledge to
become economically self-sufficient and independent?" My
answer is: "I firmly believe, the Chaco Indian has all the
potential necessary for development. And there is evidence
to support this."

"Well then, if the potential capabilities are there,
what are the prospects of success in the program?" My answer
this time is: "I do not know. It depends on so many things.
But I am sure there must be a number of promising possibilities
and opportunities that have not yet been explored." And that,
I think, is a challenge.

For example, when MEDA (Mennonite Economic Development
Association) offered a $9,000 loan on a low interest rate to
the Indian settlements a few years ago, the MEDA people had
two things in mind. First, create a fund for small loans to
individual farmers, and second, to teach them to deal with
money. A special Indian commission was to be responsible for
the administration and operation of this credit system. At
first, many Mennonite people voiced serious concern about the
wisdom of such undertaking. How would an illiterate Indian,
who could not even count correctly up to one hundred, grasp
the idea about interest rates? Well, a year later some
Indians were asked about their understanding of interest.
Their answer was something like this: Interest on loans is
like the kids of the old goat. The kids should be killed
right away, because if you don't kill them, they will grow
up and become big, and they will eat up everything you have.
Well, they got the idea all right!

Education
    Education has been a part of the program since the first
beginning of missionary work. The first objective of schooling
was to be able to read the Bible.

By now it is a well known fact, that education is a very
important factor in the process of development. In 1971
about one thousand children were taught in thirty schools
by thirty-three Indian teachers. Indian schools teach only
the first two grades so far, and there is a high rate of failure to pass grades, mainly due to insufficient training of

the teachers themselves. In addition there is a boarding
school of high standards in Yalve Sanga. Well trained teachers
teach up to the sixth grade here. Workers and leaders for
the different programs as well as teachers are getting their
basic education here.

The question is: "Is grade school education, and education of children only, enough?" It is felt that more adult
education and extension work is a necessity in the struggle
for development. And Indians today are very eager to learn.
They have a great confidence in the Mennonites and they would
like to learn everything they know. I hope that Wilmer Stahl,
an original Chaco boy and the newly appointed developmental
anthropologist, will accept the challenge and will help to
do something more in this direction.

Health

True health means complete physical, emotional and
spiritual well being and not just absence of disease. Health
has also been one of the goals of the Indian program.

When I came to the program in September, 1968, there
were already small clinics or health posts established in
each of the settlements, with a nurse in charge of each of
them. The nurses, very dedicated, did the best they could.
But because they were completely on their own for all practical purposes, they were not able to handle the situation
and the health picture was bleak. TB was completely out of
control and was the cause of death in about 40% of all deaths.
Malnutrition associated with diarrhea and respiratory infec-
tions in small children was responsible for another 40% of
the deaths. The overall mortality rate was high, and the
birth rate was high. Many parents were worried about this.
They felt they just had not enough food around for so many
children. Most of the people had hookworm and were anemic
to some degree. And sick persons cannot work at full capacity,
and it is very hard for sick people to be productive.

I felt very frustrated during the first year because of
the overwhelming health problems and the very limited resources available to deal with them.

Through valuable assistance from Holland we were finally
able to set up a very effective TB program. The death rate
from TB is diminishing already, and practically all new cases
receive proper treatment and most of them get well again.
It can be predicted that five years from now, TB will not
be a major public health problem any more. Through intensive health education, Indians are well aware of the problems
associated with TB and they cooperate very nicely.

Similarly hookworm disease will be under control soon.
Here a few specially trained Indian health workers are the
agents for change. And we have observed that once they

understand the disease and the problems involved, they often
do a better job in passing on this knowledge to their people
as the nurses or I possibly could.

Little over a year ago an intensive program was launched
to correct the malnutrition of the pre-school children. So
far attention has been focused largely on education of the
mothers in the right selection and preparation of infant
food. This program starts to show promising results. But
more needs to be done, especially in the line of food production.

The overall approach has become more and more community
oriented, with emphasis on preventing diseases. The community
is the patient and not just the one who comes to the clinic.
This helps to stretch the very scarce "health dollar" much
farther and gives much better long term results.

The nurses spend a considerable part of their time in
health education. It is planned to train more and more
Indian auxiliaries and turn the responsibility over to them
wherever possible. But the more we do, more problems we see.
That is a challenge. Besides, for everything we wanted to
do or had to do, the necessary funds had to come from some-
where. So it always has been reassuring to us to know we
were not alone, there were other people who cared. Many a
gift has shown this to workers in the program. It is a real
challenge to be instrumental to the development of a searching
and struggling society.

The Indian Church

Established already for many years, it has had and is
having a positive influence on the development of the society.
Nevertheless there are some questions about the actual leadership. There is the question of dealing with today's young
generation, for example. It seems that the church needs
better trained leaders who would be able to deal better with
the questions of rapid social change and would be able to
interpret these changes in the light of Biblical teaching.

The role of the missionary is changing and will have to
change even more. His role will be that of a teacher and
advisor. A healthy and spiritually active church will be
essential to the future of the Indians.

Let us come back for a moment to the question: "Why
did Mennonites become involved in this long range program
with the Indians?"

First and above all, they felt God's calling on them,
go and do something. And they wanted to obey that calling.
Reading the Bible, we will find that we are asked again and
again to go, to do, to love, to share, to care. In Hebrews
13:15 we read: "Do not neglect to do good and to share what
you have, for such sacrifices are pleasing to God."

There are other reasons:

Chaco Mennonites have been the recipients of long term international assistance in their development. Now that they are better off, why not pass on assistance to others in need as an attitude of gratitude.

Indians have almost always been the disadvantaged and exploited in the history of the Western Hemisphere. Why not make a turn and reverse the trend as a contribution to Justice?!

Mennonites and Indians in the Chaco live in the same geographic area. They have no choice as to interact. And the nature of this interaction in the future will depend largely on the nature of the interaction today. So their future fate is somehow tied together. Why are Mennonites in Canada and in the U.S. involved in outreach programs over the world? This you will have to answer for yourselves. I would just like to make one point. It is very hard for a church to stay spiritually alive without being actively involved in some kind of outreach program. That is what Christianity is all about: "Go, and...."

Conclusions

Will the Indian program in the Chaco be successful?

Well, it depends. Nobody really knows. There are no foolproof answers to the question of development. And by the way, what does successful actually mean?

All we can say today is we think we are in the right direction. But there is ample room for improvement. I feel there are good chances that with intensive continuous effort the Indian population will experience a rapid change for the better in the next decade.

I would like to conclude this with a remark Orie Miller made in 1968 about the Indian situation in the Chaco: "It is not a problem, it is a challenge." This reflects an attitude about problem solving, which can make a big difference. So let us conclude: It is not a problem, it is a challenge - to all of us.

6.
Russia (the USSR) Revisited

In the 1950's MCC made many attempts to renew contacts with Russia and to understand what was happening in that country; special interest, of course, focused on Mennonite and other Christian groups. Various proposals for contact and service were made; few of them were ultimately successful.

Reading 48

Excerpts, Proposal for a Goodwill Team to Russia and the Orient, by Paul Peachey. Presented at Executive Committee Meeting, October 1, 1955.

For some few years individuals who have been on the frontiers of our peace witness have felt at times of acute international tension that as nonresistant Christians we should be doing more to dispel the fear and suspicion that settles like a thick cloud over the peoples of the earth. Precisely as nonresistant Christians we have, it would seem, both the possibility and responsibility to refuse to accept the "iron curtain" as definitive.

In MCC work in Europe we were always restrained from attempting contact with the Russians by the knowledge that because of MCC refugee work we were on Russia's black list. Furthermore, with so many people in our constituency involved personally or by family connections in suffering inflicted by the Red revolution and regime, too many seemed unprepared for friendly gestures. In the light of this suggestions which were actually put forward were accorded cold receptions.

During last spring's Formosan crisis, out of an exchange between Harold Sherk and myself, the proposal grew that we try to send a goodwill team to Russia and the Orient through the Historic Peace Churches association, a team that would travel as a praying and witnessing Christian community or church. It was recognized that the major difficulty would be to find persons out of the Friends-Brethren-Mennonite constituencies who could be united into such a team on an evangelical basis. The advantage of such a team would be to make it less a Mennonite undertaking, so far as Russian objections might be concerned, and to make it less "sectarian" in its message.

Orie Miller, as our representative on the HPC continuation

committee, indicated his interest in carrying the matter to
that committee. Meanwhile we discovered that the several
year old attempt of the Friends to send a team had materialized
and that they are now underway under the leadership of Clarence
Pickett. Further discussion strengthened the feeling that
the proposal was vulnerable at two points in particular:
(A) the difficulty of constituting an evangelical HPC team,
and (b) the possibility that Russian authorities might feel
we are trying to pull a fast one by flying the HPC flag.

A further complicating factor is the growing interest
among some people in trying to contact Mennonites still remaining in Russia. I understand that explorations along
this line have not yet led to positive results. Nevertheless this aspect of the question would have to be borne in
mind.

As a result of further discussion and reflection I would
like to present the following two proposals to the Peace
Problems Committee.

A. A Goodwill Team

1. That American and Canadian Mennonites take steps
(on some basis other than via MCC) toward sending a team of
about six Mennonite men on a six-month tour to Russian
and other European countries in the Soviet sphere of influence, to China, Japan, India, and other far eastern
countries.

2. The objectives of this team would be: (a) To dispel distrust and to spread goodwill among the common people
through personal and communit contact. (b) To identify the
Christian message as one of love and reconciliation. (c) To
seek out Christians for fellowship and witness. (d) To aid
in the missionary witness wherever possible, particularly as
the team itself would be a witnessing, serving, praying
church. (e) To give aid to nonresistant churches and missionaries, at their request and discretion, in the strengthening of their peace witness. (f) To carry a "non-political"
witness to political persons as opportunity presents itself.
(g) To carry from our brotherhood expressions of goodwill as
would grow from a prior period of repentance and prayer
which would be encouraged throughout our entire brotherhood.
(h) To give expression to the universal character of the
Christian community which rises about national and radical
differences. (A non-white member or members of the team
would be a definite asset.) (i) To bring to our people first
hand information that would aid us in assessing the biased
reporting on which we are forced to depend and to broaden
our understanding and vision of world need and our own shortcomings.

3.   Prerequisites for tour members would likely be previous foreign experience, a background knowledge and interest
in the larger contemporary Christian and political issues,
an objective insight into the sins of our own political
and economic system and the ability to dissociate one's thinking from a pro-western outlook (without becoming gullible
in the other direction), a clear and thorough commitment to
Christian discipleship, etc. If possible, the team should
include people from various walks of life, though the above
qualifications would tend to narrow the selection to persons
in the academic fields...

*   *   *

MCC thus began a renewed effort to enter and learn about
Russia.

Reading 49
Excerpts, Minutes of Executive Committee Meeting, October 1,
1955.

In the light of the discussion /of Paul Peachey's pro-
posal/ of the previous evening, it was moved and passed to
adopt the following action as prepared by H. S. Bender and
William T. Snyder pursuant to the instructions of the evening
meeting:
a.   That a delegation be sent to Russia to visit the
Mennonites there, the size, personnel and itinerary and other
related matters to be left for later decision.
b.   That efforts on behalf of the Mennonites in Russia
as representing the interests of the Mennonites of Canada,
the United States, and South America, be coordinated, the
coordination to be through the MCC.
c.   That the MCC Executive Committee continue the ex-
ploratory work necessary in this matter, hoping that final
decision can be taken at the MCC annual meeting.
d.   That announcement concerning this matter be made
to our people in Canada, U.S.A., and South America through
the Mennonite press.
e.   That Paul Peachey's proposal for a peace testimony
and goodwill delegation to the Eastern European and Far Eastern
areas be referred to the Peace Section for careful study and
further report.

*   *   *

In 1956 an MCC delegation, led by H. S. Bender, did
visit the USSR. On his return, Bender submitted a series of
eight "Recommendations Regarding Future Contacts with Mennonites in Russia" and plans were made for another group to
go in 1957, but this visit did not materialize. During 1956

MCC had its first contact with Russian Christians when it
hosted briefly five Russian Baptists who were visiting American Baptist churches.

Reading 50
Excerpts, Minutes of Executive Committee Meeting, December 15,
1956.

H. S. Bender presented formally the report of the delegation to Russia... He submitted a series of eight "Recommendations Regarding Future Contacts with Mennonites in
Russia" as follows:

a. That the direction of these contacts be assumed by
the Mennonite Central Committee with the cooperation and
support of the Canadian Board and the European Mennonite Relief Committee including Bijzondere Nooden.

b. That a continuing program of visits and contacts be
maintained as much as possible, with one visit per year,
usually of a delegation of 2-4 persons; the October 26-
November 16 visit to be considered the first step.

c. That the next visit be immediately following the
next World Conference and as from it, ca. August 19-September
5, 1957.

d. That thorough preparation be made for this visit,
through preparation of comprehensive information about the
location and church status of the Mennonites of Russia, and
through negotiations with the Russian Baptists and proper
Russian authorities, as well as by correspondence with Mennonites in Russia, so that a precise and governmentally approved
itinerary may be developed in advance, with Mennonites in
Russia from other places to be invited to meet the group at
several strategic points.

e. That the 1957 delegation be so constituted as to
have the utmost appeal to the Russian authorities for approval,
including essentially chief Mennonite leadership from several
countries with large press representation, and large representation of Mennonites born in Russia, 15 to 20 in size.

f. That close collaboration be maintained with the
Baptists in Russia.

g. That a comprehensive and scientific report be prepared by April 1, 1957, on the location and spiritual and
church conditions of the Mennonites in Russia, based largely
upon a digest of the information contained in letters coming
out of Russia and the report of the 1956 delegation.

h. That an office be established under MCC administration for Russian Mennonite affairs, with a specially qualified person, chosen in consultation with the Canadian Board,
whose duties shall be (1) to prepare the above report and
a continuous reporting service, (2) to supervise the card

index file work and Suchdienst at Akron, Saskatoon and
Frankfurt, (3) with necessary collaboration with European
agencies, especially Evangelisches Hilfswerk in Stuttgart,
(4) also contacts in Russia. This person could also be the
MCC general director in Europe, and would in a sense be a
successor to C. F. Klassen.

*   *   *

Orie O. Miller made a commissioner trip to the USSR in
1958. Early in 1959 a major effort was made to delineate
MCC's East-West task. A set of policy guidelines was adopted.

Reading 51
Excerpts, Minutes of the Executive Committee Meeting, May 2,
1959.

NOTE: The first session of the Executive Committee
meeting was devoted to consideration of the East-West task
of the MCC, i.e., basically, what can be done and who ought
to do it, in regard to fellowship with and aid to the Mennonites and other related Christian groups in the USSR today.
For this session the Canadian Mennonites were invited to
send up to 20 representatives to attend the meeting. At a
meeting of the Canadian Mennonite Board of Colonization and
the Mennonite Central Relief Committee of Canada at Saskatoon,
J. J. Thiessen and C. A. DeFehr, both MCC members, were appointed to represent the Mennonites of Western Canada, particularly to give voice to the counsel of the above two groups
on these matters. In addition MCC members directly interested
were invited to attend; C. J. Rempel was the only one to respond and participate. The Mission Board Secretaries present
at the previous day's Conjoint meeting were also invited to
participate in the discussion.
     1. Executive Secretary Wm. T. Snyder introduced the
subject of East-West work for review and consideration in
the meeting... The chief purpose of the meeting is to arrive
at an understanding on objectives and procedures in East-
West work. O. O. Miller, Peter J. Dyck, J. J. Thiessen,
C. A. DeFehr, and Wm. T. Snyder were asked to speak on the
subject.
     2. O. O. Miller impressions on the Soviet Union from
his trip in 1958: (1) The Baptist Church is a living, working
Christian Church with a certain amount of freedom under re-
strictions; (2) Mennonites are re-settling in urban areas,
in fairly good economic circumstances, probably better off
economically than most Mennonites in Paraguay, with prospect
of rising living standards, and grouping together in clusters.
The older folks and some of the younger people are eager to

find a spiritual home, forming informal meeting groups, with
some finding satisfaction in the Baptist fellowship; (3) There
is some interest in religion among the new generation in the
Soviet Union (this observation based on a limited spot-check)...
He again explained why the Moscow Baptist leadership feels
they cannot directly work on registration for the Mennonites
by going along with Mennonites to the Ministry of Cults, the
chief reason being that they do not know the Mennonites well
enough to represent them (for example, they had heard that
some Mennonite youths in Karaganda are joining the Komsomol,
the Communist youth organization). O. O. Miller still feels
that the Baptists would assist the Mennonites in working on
registration...

   3. Peter J. Dyck. Sources of Information. His information is not based on personal contacts in Russia, but on
contacts with people from the Soviet Union, East-West meetings
such as the peace meeting in Frankfurt in January between
western and Iron Curtain theologians, newspapers from Russia
(such as Neues Leben, the German edition of Pravda), and
correspondence from Russian Mennonites with relatives in
the West. The Frankfurt and Akron offices do not correspond
directly with anyone in the Soviet Union. The Frankfurt
office also subscribes to a clipping and translating service
on things published in the Soviet Union, securing thereby
all material relating to religion in Russia. The information·
secured through this route indicates that urgent attempts
are being made to whip up flagging zeal in Russia on anti-
religious propaganda...

   5. J. J. Thiessen. The Canadians, whom he represents,
feel that foreign Mennonites should not intervene in the
matter of registration of the Mennonite church in the Soviet
Union. If the Mennonites there are interested in registration
we should encourage them, but otherwise do nothing in taking
the initiative with the ministry. There may be danger of
providing the government to take measures against the Mennonites. The Canadians are not against visits to our people
in the Soviet Union, in fact would encourage it, but not to
serve as advisers or as mediators on approaches to the government. He feels that there may be dangers of further pressure
and loss of freedom if they are registered.

   6. C. A. DeFehr, agrees with Thissen, feeling that
even the Baptists should not be asked to intervene for Mennonites. The only thing we could do would be to have private
conversations with our leaders in the Soviet Union and encourage them to consider advantages and disadvantages of registration, but they decide what to do. C. A. DeFehr stated
it is important to encourage the leaders of the Mennonite
church in their work. He also called attention to the fact
that conditions have looked good before in the Soviet Union

and we should not be too optimistic about improvement that
can be observed today.

7.   Peter J. Dyck reported B. B. Janz's opinion that
registration at this time would not only be undesirable, but
would be dangerous...

RESOLUTION ON EAST-WEST PROGRAM AND POLICIES
Adopted at a Conjoint Meeting of the MCC Executive Committee
and Representatives of the Canadian Mennonites
Chicago, Illinois, May 2, 1959

After thorough consideration of our Mennonite East-West
program and problems relating to it, and with sincere appreciation for the counsel of the Canadian brethren represented at the Saskatoon meeting of April 2, 1959, as reported
by J. J. Thiessen and C. A. DeFehr, as well as the thorough
report given by Peter J. Dyck as director of the current
East-West program, along with other reports, we adopt the
following statement of conclusions regarding the objectives
and guiding policies for the East-West program.

1.   That the strengthening of the remnant of our
Mennonite brotherhood in the Soviet Union as a true Church
of Christ and as an instrument of God for evangelism and
church-building in the USSR, in the historic Mennonite faith,
is and should continue to be a united concern and goal of
our North American Mennonite Brotherhood; and that we assist
our Russian brethren in their work as may be possible and
advisable.

2.   That we believe that our Mennonite brotherhood everywhere, along with other Christians, has the obligation of
evangelism in the USSR in the carrying out of the Great Commission; that our mission agencies be encouraged to seek
ways and means to fulfill this obligation; and that the radio
ministry of the Gospel to the Soviet Union in both Russian
and German languages as is carried on by such agencies as
the Gospel Light Hour and the Mennonite Hour be encouraged
and supported by our people as one means to this end.

3.   That a continuing program of contact, visits, encouragement, and aid for our Mennonite brethren in the Soviet
Union be maintained on behalf of the Mennonite brotherhood
in North America; and that the Mennonite Central Committee
be considered to be the responsible agency for this work.

4.   That the Mennonite brotherhood in other continents
such as South America and Europe be encouraged to share in
this concern and work, and that the Mennonite Central Committee stand ready to help them in this participation and to
represent them as they may desire.

5.   That the counsel of our Canadian brethren of more
recent Russian background be regularly solicited regarding

the various procedures and measures to be undertaken, in view of their direct relation to and deep concern for the Mennonites in the Soviet Union.

6. That in working on behalf of our brethren in the USSR, counsel and assistance be sought wherever it can be found; that the help of the Evangelical Christian-Baptist Church in the Soviet Union as already given be appreciatively acknowledged, and that we continue to seek its counsel and help.

7. That while there may be both advantages and disadvantages for the Mennonite Church in the USSR to become registered with the Soviet government, we believe this matter should be the responsibility of the Mennonites in Russia to decide, and that we stand ready to help and encourage them in whatever decision they may make in this matter, subject to their desires.

8. That the reuniting of broken families either outside or inside the Soviet Union continue to be a vital concern and goal for the Mennonite Central Committee and the Canadian Mennonite agencies as long as the need continues.

9. That it is our obligation to be fully informed about the state of the Mennonites in the Soviet Union and that the work of the East-West Information Service (Suchdienst) be strengthened to increase its usefulness to any enlargement of future service to our Russian brethren, this to be on a practical basis.

10. That we urge the Canadian brotherhood to make available strong leaders to share in future delegations or visits to the Soviet Union.

11. That the Mennonite Central Committee attempt to send a delegation to the Soviet Union either this coming autumn or the following spring, including contacts with both Mennonites and Evangelical Christian-Baptists in the program of the delegation.

12. That a special Supplementary Parcel Fund be established in the relief fund for the purpose of assisting needy Mennonites now living in the Western Hemisphere (principally Paraguay) to send parcels to relatives in the Soviet Union, this to be an imprest fund to be replenished as needed.

13. That the East-West office continue to explore all possibilites for sending Bibles and Christian literature to Mennonites and others in the Soviet Union.

14. That we continue to have an interest in a Christian testimony and possible relief work (including parcel service) in such countries as Poland, Czechoslovakia, Hungary, and Yugoslavia.

*   *   *

In 1960 H. A. Fast, Gerhard Lohrenz, Peter Dyck and David Wiens visited Russia under MCC auspices, and in 1966

William Snyder, Frank Peters, and David Neufeld joined an American Baptist delegation which visited Russian Baptist churches.

Reading 52
Excerpts, Report on the Visit to the Soviet Union, by David P. Neufeld. Presented at Executive Committee Meeting, December 16-17, 1966.

"Dave, this is Russia", said William Snyder as our plane descended to land on the runway of Moscow's international airport. We had been waiting for this moment for a long time. In the fall of 1965 there were some hopes of a delagation of Baptists and Mennonites going to visit the Russian Christians, but it didn't materialize. The proposed April-May, 1966 visit also did not materialize, and for the last week we had been anxiously waiting for visas which actually arrived only the day prior to our leaving.

When a Russian Baptist delegation visited the American Baptists in 1964, they were also able to visit large Mennonite churches. At a meeting in the Alexanderwohl Church in Kansas, Rev. Ivan Motorin invited the Mennonites to join the next American Baptist delegation to the Soviet Union. At the time he enthusiastically spoke of arrangements to visit Mennonite Communities, and to show us the life and work of the Russian Baptist churches. As it was expected, he was unable to make good on some of the promises, but it must always be said to the credit of the Russian Baptists, that they treated us royally and did everything they could for us...

PURPOSE OF THE DELEGATION
1. To know the Baptist Church in Russia. It is not simple to be officially recognized as a church by the Government of the Soviet Union. Our impression is that the Government wants as few groups as possible to deal with. The result is that the protestant churches have created the Union of Evangelicals-Baptists, which has official Government recognition. Belonging to the Union are Baptists, Evangelicals, Pentecostals and Mennonites. However, the Baptists form the bulk of the membership. Seeing that more and more of the Mennonites in Russia are joining the Union it becomes imperative that the rest of the Mennonites in the world need to know the Russian Baptists better.
2. A second objective was to encourage the Christians in the Soviet Union. This was even more necessary than we had first visualized. When one is cut off from the rest of the world for so long there is a real danger that one considers himself to be as Elijah: "I, even I only remain a

prophet of the Lord". We asked the brethren in Irkustk
when they last had been visited be American Christians.
"Never" was the answer.

3. A third objective was to visit Mennonite communities,
to fellowship with the fellow believers and to find out what
their joys and sorrows consisted of.

Well, our encounters with the Russian people immediately
began when we got off the Royal Dutch Airlines plane. The
customs waved us through. The Church leaders of the Moscow
church were there to meet us with taxis prepared to take us
to the Leningradskaja Hotel. After the brief moment in our
rooms we were called down for the reception dinner. This
was to become the prototype of all Russian hospitality which
finds expression in much eating. Caviar, sturgeon fish,
smoked salmon and cold meat cuts were designed to whet the
appetite for three more courses to follow: salenka soup,
meat and potatoes and a dessert. During the coming weeks
we learned that Russian hospitality simply insisted on much
eating. We begged for smaller portions, for fewer courses,
for fewer calories, but to no avail. Be our guests! Eat
up!...

I felt at home among the Russian Baptists. They look
so much like Mennonites! When we tried to determine which
were the Mennonites in the Irkutsk congregation I was unable
to find them, despite the fact that I knew there were some
there. Besides, it seems that in the long period of our
forefather's sojourn in that land they took up many of the
Russian customs. When the preachers spoke, they seemed to
have the same lilt in their voice as many of my older co-
workers. The gestures of head and hands also seemed to be
strongly familiar. When the deacon received the offering,
he held a little sack into which the Kopeks were dropped.
Where had I seen that before? When announcing a hymn the
minister would read a verse, then it was sung, read another,
and it was sung. This surely was partly due to the shortage
of hymnaries, but there was something strangely familiar about
it too. Besides the Russians use a host of Plattdeutsch
words such as Oza for Lake; Paletou for overcoat; Poyas for
belt and Shimadaun for suit case!

I never knew why my father was so terribly insistent on
building a picket fence around our farm home. Now I know.
Every home, no matter how poor, in the Russian village has
a picket fence. It's simply a must.

Theologically, the Baptists are strongly evangelical.
Salvation, personal piety, prayer, brotherly love are upper-
most in their thinking. They take the Bible literally. Their
preaching is simple. Yet their services are deeply emotional.
We asked them about their teaching escatology. They have
little to say, it seems, about the final judgment.

THE MENNONITES

We constantly keep our ears open to learn all we could about the Mennonites in Russia. The Baptists estimate that there are 40,000 Mennonites in Russia: 20,000 Mennonite Brethren and 20,000 "Church" Mennonites. Some estimates claim the total number to be 50,000. 16,000 Mennonites have joined the Baptist Church and should be considered as Baptists, though our brethren would hardly admit that.

When we arrived in Russia we soon found out that it would not be possible for us to go to places where there are concentrations of Mennonites. This was a big disappointment. When we shared the concern with the 8 Mennonite church leaders they said: "Don't be too disappointed, because if you would have gone to one or two Mennonite communities, you wouldn't have met so many representatives from all across Russia." This meant, of course, that we had to make the most of the half day meeting and consequent private meetings on the day of Rev. Zhidkov's funeral. The men who came were: Johan Penner, G. C., Frunse; Jacob Fast, M.B., Novasibirsk; A. Friesen, M.B., Karaganda; Traugott Quiring, M.B., Duschanbe; Johann Martens, M.B., Kant near Frunse; Friedrich Funk, M.B., Duschanbe; Peter Heese, G.C., Tokmak; Helmut Kliewer, M.B., Kant; and Victor Kreiger, M.B., Moscow.

These men traveled 2,000 miles and more to get to Moscow, but they were eager to meet with us, to share, ask questions. We asked them to each give a brief report of their church, which they did. They reported how God had touched Russia with a sweeping revival in the 1950's...

When we went to Irkutsk in Siberia we had the hope that we might meet some Mennonites there. When we asked the minister upon our arrival if any Mennonites worshipped with the Baptists, he informed us that some 50 German speaking people were members of the church. Imagine our joy when that evening we met with brothers and sisters in this capital of the exiled masses of the past. "There are Mennonites all over Siberia", they said, "not in large numbers, but sprinkled in many areas."

What are the needs among the Mennonites? Just as among the Baptists the need is for Bibles, hymnbooks, choir numbers, books on theology. There is also need for encouragement. The men wanted to know whether we consider them to be way off the beaten track. So don't give up writing letters, sending gifts.

SOME CONCLUSIONS

There are many things which one can conclude after such a brief visit, but cannot be sure if all of them are valid:

1.   The words of Christ about the church are true:

"the gates of hell shall not prevail against it."
2. The Baptist church is a growing evangelical force
in Russia.
3. The Baptist-Mennonite relationships seems to be
satisfactory on both sides.
4. The "Church Mennonites" will probably seek to retain
the Mennonite church in Russia by seeking registration with
the Government.
5. Mennonite church leadership is made up largely of
middle-aged and younger men.
6. Both Mennonites and Baptists are theologically
conservative.
7. It is becoming easier for the church in Russia.
8. There is hope for more communication with the west.
This was the first official delegation visit made by
Mennonites to the Soviet Union. It has significance. The
Mennonite leaders caught it quickly when they said: "Brethren,
think of what this will mean to our churches when we tell
them: We have seen the brethren from America. This is an
historic event where the contact between East and West had
been restored."

*   *   *

In the late 60's and early 70's increased contact with
the Soviet Union was possible. MCC personnel visited periodically, and representatives of Russian churches occasionally
visited the United States. In 1973 Walter Sawatsky was
appointed MCC representative at the Centre for the Study of
Religion and Communism near London. MCC began to take a
greater role in encouraging studies of Russian Mennonite
history and commemorations of significant historical events.
The following readings illustrate some of these involvements.

Reading 53
Excerpts, Minutes of Executive Committee Meeting, May 23,
1968.

12. BAPTIST-MENNONITE RELATIONSHIP IN SOVIET UNION
Adolfs Klaupiks, Relief Coordinator of the Baptist World
Alliance, summarized his report of his visit to the Soviet
Union in March, 1968. He commented on the division within
the Baptist Church in the Soviet Union. A group of dissenters,
according to Klaupiks, which anticipated securing support
from the West and achieving positive results in a short time
is now somewhat less active because neither the support nor
the results were forthcoming. The leaders of the Russian
Baptist Church are deeply concerned about the division which
has developed. The Baptist World Alliance views the problem
as an internal one which needs to be solved within the Soviet

Union. Some Mennonites are also involved in the divisions.
In some instances Mennonites have been active in reconciliation
between the dissenting and the mainstream groups. Of the
202 persons imprisoned for religious activity, a few have
been released. A Bible school has been started in Moscow
with 100 persons accepted from 300 qualified applicants.
Bibles and hymn books in limited quantities are to be printed
and new members are being added to the churches. Church
registration with the government seems to be carried out more
smoothly than earlier. Conversions are taking place quietly
in many places.

Reading 54
Excerpts, Minutes of Executive Committee Meeting, July 23,
1969.

Peter Dyck reported on the visit of the five representatives from the Soviet Union (four Baptists and one Mennonite)
to Canadian Baptist and Mennonite churches from June 9-30,
1969. Peter Dyck and Adolfs Klaupiks accompanied the visitors, and the tour ended on July 1 at Akron. Audiences
totalling over 20,100 were reached. The trip was without
incident of any kind and the delegation left with new insights and very grateful for the opportunity and the encounter.
It is suggested that for the next fraternal exchange, a
seminar might be planned. This could possibly be a year from
now for perhaps ten days to two weeks in Moscow or Leningrad.
The brethren from the Soviet Union suggested the theme might
be, "The Nature and Mission of the Church," including also
something on training for leadership and membership. William
Snyder indicated that we would need to discuss this with the
Baptist World Alliance for possible joint participation.

Reading 55
Excerpts, Minutes of Executive Committee Meeting, September
24-25, 1975.

20. EUROPE-NORTH AFRICA
a. Peter J. Dyck, director of the Europe-North Africa
program, spoke of meaningful contacts with Mennonites in
Europe including an excellent annual retreat at the Bienen-
berg.
b. Approximately 30 to 50 persons continue to come per
month from Russia and thus the work among the Umsiedler
grows. Peter reviewed the personnel needs and building projections for the Umsiedler. Efforts are planned to document
the history of the Mennonites from the time of the Communist
takeover in Russia to the present. Walter Sawatsky will
lead this project.

7.

The Story of MCC Canada

MCC Canada has become an integral part of world-wide MCC activities. While relief committees were at work in Canada long before World War II, it was only in 1943 that steps were taken to coordinate their work in a Canadian MCC office, which was considered a regional or sub-office of MCC Akron.

Reading 56

Report of and Recommendations from Sittings in Ottawa, December 8-9, 1943.

The six Canadian brethren present (Representatives of the three Canadian Relief Committees whose constituencies support M.C.C.-W.S.R. and the Ontario Conference of Historic Peace Churches) expressed appreciation for the reports of M.C.C. relief activities and plans given by Bennett and Miller, and stated that they felt their groups were minded to continue using these channels of relief services in a growing way and seemed to agree that an M.C.C. office in Canada could facilitate and make more efficient this effort--particularly initially in the following areas:

    1.   In coordinating and assisting in servicing the clothing gifts efforts.

    2.   In relief work information service to Churches in Canada.

    3.   In coordinating, holding and forwarding of funds to the several areas for which designated.

    4.   To assist in coordinated liaisonship with Canadian Foreign Relief services and agencies.

    5.   To assist in channelizing Canadian Relief workers to the points of needed service.

Miller and Bennett stated that subject to confirmation by M.C.C. Executive Committee an M.C.C. office would probably be set up within the next two months, and that Toronto was first in mind as a location.

    1.   That a staff of three for same was in mind--A Director, A Sister to be in charge of clothing, A Clerk, and that suggestions for these posts would be appreciated.

    2.   That Bennett would likely represent M.C.C. in finally locating and setting up this office and staffing it.

Miller and Bennett also stated that 3 or 4 additional workers were immediately contemplated to England with the

hope that a registered nurse and perhaps a man or woman qualified as cook and dietitian for work with boys could come from Canada. Nominations for these places are solicited.
   Miller and Bennett also invited the submission from all the groups of relief worker availabilities--stating that the M.C.C. post-war program was being planned and developed so that anyone with divine call to serve in it and who can make M.C.C. worker standards his or her own would be used. It was also mentioned that the total M.C.C.-W.S.R. program is being based on an estimated 1944 income of $350,000 in cash and $150,000 in kind, the cash representing an average of $2 per church member from all M.C.C. supporting constituencies for the year.

Reading 57
Excerpt, MCC Executive Committee Minutes, December 30, 1943.

   8. After an interview with Brother and Sister Jesse Short, it was agreed to appoint them to take over the work of the Canadian M.C.C. office beginning January 1 and continuing until a permanent director of the office, possibly Cornelius Rempel, can be secured or at least to April 1.

Reading 58
Excerpt, MCC Executive Committee Meeting, February 26, 1944.

   25. Ernest Bennett reported on the Canadian sub-office in Kitchener, Ont., which has now been set up at 223 King Street East. On recommendation of Ernest Bennett it was moved and passed to appoint Cornelius Rempel and wife of Kitchener as Manager and Matron of the M.C.C. Canadian headquarters at an allowance of $80.00 Canadian per month and maintenance beginning as soon as he can secure a release from the bank. Meanwhile Jesse Short and wife will continue. Additional workers needed will be a clerk and a clothing depot worker. Moved and passed to authorize appointment of a clerk and clothing depot worker as soon as they can be secured.

Reading 59
Report of the Canadian Mennonite Central Committee, December, 1944.

   At the annual meeting we take time to survey our activities of the past year and we are happy for this opportunity of passing on to you a little information about the Canadian office of the Mennonite Central Committee. For a number of years the Canadian Mennonite constituencies have contributed cash and clothing for war sufferers and famine

stricken areas. The Executive's plans to plan an office
in Canada came to fruition at the end of January of this year.
During the intermittent period the office has developed from
an embryonic stage to a more mature establishment.

There are ways and means which could be employed to make
the growth and development more rapid but we think a policy
of conservatism will on the long run bring more results.
From the different contacts which we were able to make and
the thoughts which have been expressed to us, we have now
come to the conclusion that the cautious uncertain steps
which were characteristic of our early existance could perhaps be replaced by those of a more definite nature.

The Clothing Depot - The growth of the Kitchener
Clothing is not as startling as that of Ephrata and Newton.
Several reasons are these: lack of adequate clothing among
many Western farmers, the change for the Eastern Mennonite
constituencies from contributing new clothing to the Non-
resistant Relief Organization, the ready outlet for any used
clothing in Northern Saskatchewan and the lack of information
and realization of the importance of this phase of relief
work. We feel confident that the appointment of Sister
Clara Snider who not only is an efficient worker but one who
is well-known to the Canadian sewing circles, the distribution of the relief clothing folders in both the English
and German language and the proposed visit of Sister Lydia
Lehman will go a long way in making us more relief conscious.
November and December have shown a very decided increase in
both interest and contributions and we firmly believe that
future growth will be more rapid.

Relief Workers - A further duty of the Canadian office
is to look for the proper workers to be sent to the various
fields and then to be helpful in securing their necessary
papers. Four Canadians have left Canada this year. Mabel
Cressman and Vernon Toews are now in England, J. Harold Sherk
is on his way to India and Arthur Jahnke is now at Akron
ready to leave for Egypt. Barring some unfortunate developments, two more workers will leave Canada before very long.

Publicity - Through personal contact and by way of monthly
publications, we try to keep the Canadian Mennonites posted
on what is happening in the relief fields as well as to present the need as we find it in the world today. It has been
very gratifying to us to visit the different churches and
annual conferences and be asked for more information. One
man after hearing that the Canadian office was opened to be
of more service explained "You can serve us best by giving
us more and more information." The British relief angle has
been stressed so much that many districts and communities are
of the opinion that the MCC directed relief consists of one
field only, that in England. We have seen whole conferences

become relief conscious after hearing of the aims and motives
of Mennonite relief and hearing of the different fields and
their activities.

After studying the work in Canada, we can truly say
with Paul, "Now unto Him who is able to do exceedingly above
all that we ask or think...unto Him be glory."

Sincerely yours,
C. J. Rempel, Manager

Reading 60
Memo of Understanding Regarding Procedures To Apply Between
Akron, Kitchener, and Winnipeg.   MCC Executive Committee
Meeting, March 24, 1945.

I.   Relief Worker Candidacies
    1.   The MCC is ready to consider assignments to indi-
vidual members of any of our constituent groups who give
evidence of genuine Christian experiences, a call to this
service, who are in good standing in their own congregation
and can be recommended from the leaders of their group, between the ages of twenty-four and fifty, who are in good
health and without unprovided for financial obligations or
unmet responsibilities to dependents and who can heartily
subscribe to the Workers' Standards outlined in the MCC Hand-
book.   Candidates should have educational training including
high school or more or have some particular equivalent skill
such as mechanical, nursing, or etc.
    2.   Any candidate who would seem to come under the fore-
going category if writing to Akron first will be referred
to the Kitchener office and (if West of Ontario to Winnipeg) for checking on foregoing points.
    3.   Data of the candidate when completed is submitted
to Brother Byler's office, Akron.
    4.   Any individual applicant who in any one or more
points fails to meet the foregoing requirements but who for
other special reasons should be considered, is to be similarly
processed.
    5.   With the candidate's file should come a statement
from Kitchener or Winnipeg as to the prospects of the candidate's Selective Service release if appointed to service.
    6.   With Akron's approval of the candidate will come
instructions as to the candidate's processing for outgoing.
This in most cases would include a field assignment so that
Selective Service release, passport, and exit permit can be
arranged for.   A training and orientation period of from
six to twelve weeks to be arranged from Akron for Goshen
and/or Akron.
    7.   The usual procedure will probably be to take ap-

pointed workers for training and processing bi-monthly - the dates to be later arranged as convenient to Goshen College.

    8. The MCC to be responsible for processing and training expenses from the time the candidate leaves his or her home.

II. Canadian Clothing-Gathering, Processing and Shipping

    1. It is agreed that negotiations with Ottawa contemplate an over-all Mennonite permit and arrangements with Government.

    2. That as soon as Ottawa's attitude towards the present Kitchener application becomes clear, negotiations be further undertaken in terms of five tons monthly.

    3. That allocations within the total allowed be arranged on a mutually satisfactory basis between Kitchener and Winnipeg stations.

    4. That these stations to the extent practically possible arrange for uniform processing procedures; also labeling, packing, recording, crediting and reporting to Akron.

    5. That directions for foreign shipments come from Akron.

    6. That particular Canadian clothing publicity from the Kitchener office be previously cleared with the constituent group affected.

    7. That Kitchener office director, Rempel, be prepared to handle all Canadian Government liaisonship affecting this program except such contacts as the constituent groups prefer to reserve to their own representatives.

III. Relief Food - Processing, Gathering and Shipping

    1. Inasmuch as such program in its totality is now in process of being worked out by John Snyder of the Akron office, the detailed procedures in Canada need to await the general announcement of plan from Akron.

    2. Following this general announcement, it is expected that Rempel of the Kitchener office will make the necessary Governmental contacts for the Canadian Mennonite program except as Canadian constituent groups desire to keep such contacts for their own group and that Rempel keep group leaders fully adivsed of the program as developed from Akron and contacts made and contemplated with Ottawa.

    3. That the Kitchener office then stand ready to cooperate with the several groups as they may request as to manner and nature of publicity, working out and handling such details as ration points, providing jars, announcing and maintaining standards of food processing, gathering at convenient centers, arranging for such centers and their operation, packaging and storing of food processed, etc.

    4. Directions for foreign shipment to come from the Akron office.

*   *   *

Four Canadian Mennonite relief and peace organizations were at work in 1944, the Mennonite Central Relief Committee, the Canadian Mennonite Relief Committee, the Conference of Historic Peace Churches, and the Non-Resistant Relief Organization. On invitation from MCC, C. F. Klassen was appointed to represent MCRC on the MCC Executive Committee in December, 1944. In May, 1946 J. J. Thiessen, Saskatoon, was added as MCRC representative on the MCC Executive Committee, and in March, 1950 B. B. Janz was appointed as additional representative of MCRC to MCC.

This pattern of representation continued essentially unchanged until 1963. In December of that year the Historic Peace Church Council of Canada (HPCCC), after considerable advance preparation, called a meeting in Winnipeg to consider possible new forms of organization and cooperation. One of the names proposed for the new agency was Canadian Mennonite Council (CMC) but the motion which was finally adopted read: "Be it, therefore, resolved that we adopt the name of 'Mennonite Central Committee (Canada)'". A preliminary constitution was adoped and elections held, with David P. Neufeld chosen as first chairman of the organization. It was agreed "That in all overseas relief the CMC/MCC Canada/ will work through MCC". It was during the course of this meeting that David P. Neufeld gave the following address:

Reading 61
Meeting, Portage Ave. M.B. Church, Winnipeg, Manitoba. December 12-14, 1963. Appendix. "My Dream About Canadian Mennonite Council".

I sit and daydream. I find it relaxing. It's not as hard as thinking and not as boring as just sitting. In this soft light of daydreams the Canadian Mennonite Council has showed up repeatedly, and its so easy to conjure up a structure of great importance and value. Because one need not always be entirely realistic, nor logical for that matter, when day dreaming, it becomes simpler to arrive at an ideal. So let me share with you some of my dreams.

My wife keeps pestering me to explain what the difference between the various relief organizations is. Patiently and with great detail I explain. The result is that she throws all my finely built structures over by simply asking "Well then CMRIC is MCC." "Well yes," I answer, and thinking it over, I add, "no, not really, you know, but CMRIC does support MCC." "Well doesn't CMRC support MCC too," she counters. "Well yes." I say, only to find that my finely woven statements were of no avail. It isn't clear yet! So, because she is the vice president of the Ladies Aid in church, she arranges to have Jake Klassen speak to them for one hour about

the relationships and interrelationships of Mennonite Relief
organization. When she got home from church she said that
now everything was clear, but I didn't dare ask her what was
clear, for I'm sure we'd have to start all over again.

I suppose this is part of the reason of why I've thought
of the Canadian Mennonite Council as being

1. A simple organization

As leaders in our congregations we still know about some
of our differences, but some of our people don't, and are not
greatly concerned either. The world needs organizations that
can get a job done with a minimum of red tape, and the church
certainly has had enough of the red stuff. CMC should be:

a. A common point of contact. As people coming from
a variety of churches, we know too little of each other. And
even if we want to learn, we don't know where to begin. CMC
could provide that contact by bringing people together in
conferences and drives for relief, in having this delegate
body of believers actively seek to promote relief from suffering
and understanding among the nations, by joint work programs
in the clothing centres and by jointly supplying the personnel for work projects.

b. The Canadian Mennonite Council would certainly sim-
plify life in that it would become a clearing house for all
inter-Mennonite undertakings. I may want to support two
orphans in Hebron, but I don't know where to send the money,
but if I send it to CMC they will see that it gets there.
Besides one must also consider that about April 1 Mr. Pearson
wants an account of our income and expenditures. Receipts
from Akron just won't be accepted as being income-tax deduc-
tible but those from CMC are.

c. Furthermore, it is my hope that CMC will introduce
and/or accept as its area of responsibility all other inter-
Mennonite activities and movements that are deemed desirable
by the brass and/or the grass of the Mennonite constituency.
The CMC should be willing to accept from the various sectors
of the Mennonite constitutency those areas of conern, service,
and witness which are best handled on an inter-Mennonite
rather than on a denominational basis.

Then too, Canadian Mennonite Council needs to be:

2. A big organization.

We hear a lot of talk in Conferences of having to work
at the "grass root" level. Certainly; depends on what you're
talking about. But if it means that in every area we should
organize to function independently, I don't believe it any
more. Business has found out, long ago, that to be effective
you must be big, else you don't make it. In our inter-Mennonite projects, and particularly in the area of relief we must
be big.

a. To cut down on the overhead.

We can't afford a fully staffed relief office in every
province! Nor can we afford to have five different promotional
programs. Mennonites and Brethren in Christ are a frugal
people who want their money to go to feed hungry people, and
not to maintain a big office and staff. Obviously we must
have some staff, or else the work doesn't get done, but
let every member count.

There was a time when distances played a large role.
That's no longer ture. Hence I fail to see why it shouldn't
be possible to administer the program from either B.C., Manitoba or Ontario.

A second reason why we need a big organization is:
b. To unify the program.

If everyone has his isolated program and knows little
of what the other is doing, there is overlapping in some
areas and a lack in others. If we have a "central intelli-
gence agency" it is possible to know in what areas we are
weak. The churches can't know, they must be told. By sending
out the necessary promotional literature and speakers, certain
needs are highlighted and alleviated. Then we have an organization that can act--and act quickly.
c. To give the organization flexibility.

Someone else will speak to the need for sections within
the organization of the Canadian Mennonite Council. The
beauty of this pattern is that each of our congregations can
share in the work of CMC in the capacity they desire. In
the formative years of CMC, I visualize that some congregations
will want the bulk of their contributions to go to overseas
relief through MCC. Quite in order, if they then work through
CMC overseas relief section. Others will want to subsidize
the program in South America heavily. It will be quite in
order to eartag contributions for this. At the beginning of
each year CMC needs to make up a budget and when eartaged
contributions come, they help to fill that part of the budget.

This will enable churches to ease into the load and interests of CMC as they find occasion and interest. Ideally,
I suppose, we would think of all churches contributing to
the general fund, which could then be dispersed according to
the budget proposed by the Board of Directors. Practically
I don't think it will work like that for a while yet.

In the third place CMC must be:
3. <u>A cooperating Organization.</u>
a. Cooperate with MCC

Mennonite Central Committee is a good thing! It has become a part of us and we don't want to give it up, much more,
strengthen it. MCC has been highly effective in the overseas relief program. There is no sense in developing our own
overseas program. It would only result in confusion and
added overhead expenditures. Just as the Canadian Bible

Society became independent of the British and Foreign Bible Society, yet acts as a subsidiary to the mother organization, so I feel CMC will continue to undergird the work of MCC. This will mean that we guard in overlapping with MCC. Whereas it will be necessary to have our own peace section in order to speak to government as a unified body, it is unnecessary that our peace section discuss the biblical imperative of Christian love independently of Akron. The theology for both nations remains the same, but the practical implications may be different.

   b. CMC will be a body seeking to retain the strength of those relief and service organizations which have now been dissolved.

   CHPC has been strong in the area of peace and witnessing to government. CMRIC has done a tremendous job in the area of immigration and Mennonite Aid. CMRC has proven that a strong appeal can be made for special projects and that the results are gratifying. We need to be conscious of these strengths and seek to retain them. This will come only if there is a strong feeling of Christian brotherliness which can result in a frank and open discussion.

   4. In some areas, an independent organization.
   To the churches the 49th parallel, which divides Canada from the USA, is insignificant. Yet we are constantly being made aware of the fact that we live in two different nations, even in our church work. If MCC, Akron could give all the service in Canada, which our churches require, there would be little need to organizing CMC. What particular needs do we have:

   a. We need a united voice.
   We need to speak to Government and to society at large as a united voice. When it comes to alternative service we need unity of purpose and program. Only so can we effectively speak to Government. CMC should become the united voice of Canadian Mennonites to society in general, and to its leaders in particular in matters of social concern.

   b. We need an inter-Mennonite rallying point in Canada. We are too divided. We must begin to rub shoulders. I'm not speaking about an organizational union, but I am speaking about an understanding of each other.

   c. We need an independent immigration program. Before many years are over Canada will admit many more immigrants. We can't keep people out, when we have so much room, and many nations have so little. Our program in the field of helping immigrants must include our own blood brothers in the first place, but it might well be extended.

   d. We need a limited independent relief program, because of our particular interest and also because of our particular opportunities. Many of our people have relatives in South

America, and feel they want to help them. MCC just sent Harvey Taves to investigate flood damage in Cuba, because he is a Canadian, and as such can go to Cuba. When a delegation goes to China it will be made up of Canadians. To work in India, it's distinct advantage to be a Canadian. I need not spell out the implications or the program, but there seems to be a validity in having a limited independent relief program.

e. We need a strong promotional program for relief that originates from Canada. If this comes from a central office it can be inexpensive and effective. CMC could well serve as an office of public relations for Mennonites, generally.

Well, I know, some of this is a bit hazy, but then, day-dreams always are.

- David P. Neufeld

*   *   *

At its next meeting, January 16, 1964, in Chicago, MCC (Canada) J. M. Klassen was invited to serve as executive-secretary "effective immediately", and accepted. One of his first assignments was to encourage provincial Mennonite and Brethren in Christ organizations to "organize as provincial bodies as soon as possible". The following report was shared with MCC at the same time:

Reading 62
Excerpts, Report to the MCC Annual Meeting, Chicago, Illinois, January 17-18, 1964.

We appreciate the opportunity to report briefly on the unification of all existing relief and service organizations into one cooperating body which will henceforth function as a unit and which is designed to speak on behalf of all Mennonite and Brethren in Christ churches in Canada.

History: Cooperative inter-Mennonite organizations and activity is nothing new in Canada, and the new organization was not born because of a lack of inter-Mennonite relief organizations. At present we have in Ontario alone six separate inter-Mennonite and Brethren in Christ supported organizations with the oldest being the NRRO which was organized in 1917 and is still functioning today, being supported by the various Mennonite and Brethren in Christ churches. In 1922 the Mennonite Board of Colonization (now known as CMRIC) was organized and supported mainly by GC and MB Mennonites. In 1941 the CMRC was organized in Manitoba being supported by the various smaller conferences not directly connected with the Mennonite Board of Colonization. No, the new body was not formed because of a lack of relief organizations, but partly because of an overabundance of them.

Over the last decade increased communication between the approximately fifteen groups has been evidenced with its natural results. Increasingly we became aware of the fact that our interests were the same and our programs not dissimilar. The first meeting of delegates was called for the fall of 1958. In 1959 the HPCC of Canada was formed and worked primarily in the area of peace, but was also the only inter-Mennonite body which could call in delegates to discuss matters of mutual concern. In September 1959 a Canada-wide meeting of representatives was called to again discuss a possible unification of program and passed a resolution calling for further study to be undertaken towards our previously defined goal. By April 1963 another conference was held and a definite decision was made to create an all-Canada relief organization under the name of "Canadian Mennonite Council." The organizational meeting was then held in December of 1963 and the name changed to "Mennonite Central Committee (Canada)."

Purpose: The purpose of the Mennonite Central Committee (Canada) shall be:

a. To function as a charitable organization in the relief of human suffering and distress, and in aiding, rehabilitating, reestablishing Mennonite and other refugees, and generally to support, conduct, maintain, and administer relief and kindred charitable projects. "To help fulfill the mission of the church in the name of Christ," the Prince of Peace.

b. To coordinate the relief, peace, and service efforts of the provincial and other organizations.

c. To operate without purpose of gain for its members.

d. To give leadership in exploring and initiating new areas of service.

e. To act as a united voice for the Canadian Mennonite brotherhood in matters of national concern, such as peace witness, alternative service, government contact, immigration, and such other matters as may be designated to it by the member conferences or organizations.

Organizational Structure: Our aim was for simplicity in structure. The findings committee of the December 1963 meeting among other things said, "The organization shall be as simple as possible and it should endeavor to bring order and system out of present confusion and proliferation of structure." Its relationship to MCC Akron will continue as heretofore with the following expressing our intentions. Our purpose is expressed in our constitution as follows:

Mennonite Central Committee (Canada) recognizes the Mennonite Central Committee (Akron) as the international relief agency for Mennonites and Brethren in Christ in Canada and United States. The Mennonite Central Committee (Canada), while operating independently of Mennonite Central Committee

Akron, shall cooperate and seek counsel with that body.

At our December 12, 1963, meeting we passed the following resolution: "That in all overseas relief the CMC will work through MCC."

It is our feeling that our full organizational structure will not be free of wrinkles within a year or two. We intend to proceed one step at a time. We believe there is a need for a peace program in Canada since Akron cannot very well represent us in Ottawa. How this will work out in the future, only time will tell. Our interest in immigration will continue on the same cooperative basis with MCC. We hope to operate two clothing processing centers with shipments overseas to continue under MCC direction.

Some Developments: The total impact of this new organization is not yet fully visualized. Some of the developments we would like to share with you as follows:

a. Executive elected was:
   Chairman - D. P. Neufeld - GC Winnipeg
   Vice-Chairman - Newton Gingerich - OM - Markham
   Secretary-Treasurer - C. J. Rempel - MB - Kitchener
   Additional Members
   E. J. Swalm - Brethren in Christ - Duntroon
   Ted Friesen - GC - Altona
   Harvey Plett - EM - Steinbach
   J. J. Thiessen - GC - Saskatoon
b. Head Office - Winnipeg, Manitoba
   Executive Secretary - appointed yesterday - J. M. Klassen - three years
   Provincial Committee - will be continuing on a strong basis and with considerable autonomy
c. Interim Period - All previous relief and service organizations were asked to continue as heretofore but work towards a complete integration by November 30, 1964.

                    *   *   *

MCC (Canada) overseas involvement continued primarily through the MCC Akron office as planned, but increasing demands came to MCC (Canada) for regional coordination of many areas, including for example, the Trainee and Self-help Programs, material aid purchases, and others. The opportunity to serve as a channel for Canadian International Development Agency (CIDA) funds and interests, which reached a total of 1.5 million dollars in 1978, led to the establishing of an Overseas Services Office in Winnipeg in 1976, as part of the total MCC (Canada) program. This office included a full-time projects officer for CIDA programs as described in the following document.

Reading 63
MCC Development Desk in Canada.   Minutes, MCC (Canada)
Executive Committee, October 24-25, 1972.

Introduction: During the past two decades, development work has grown from isolated and idealistically con-
ceived dreams to a place where it is now a recognized tool
for meeting human need in various underdeveloped nations.
This tool is being used to feed the hungry, clothe the naked,
heal the diseased, and enlighten the uninformed. The so-
called Third World or "developing" countries have seen the
value of this no-strings-attached development aid. MCC has
been a pioneer in this type of ministry. As we continue to
look at population growth, the shrinking areas of available
land for food production, the growing economic gap between
the have and the have-not nations, the increasing self-aware-
ness of the "emerging" nations, and the rising discontent
of the poverty-stricken masses, it is evident that development work should be stepped up and all available resources
should be harnessed. Because injustice and unrighteousness
as well as ignorance and helplessness are often the root
causes of these distressing situations, it falls into the mandate of the Christian disciple, and consequently the church
of Jesus Christ, to use all available opportunities and talents
in development work.
Canadian Situations: A special situation has developed
for MCC in Canada. Through the Canadian International
Development Agency's department for Non-Governmental Organizations (NGO), the Canadian government has offered the Mennonite Central Committee funds for development work. During
the past two years increasing amounts have been made available
to non-governmental organizations. In 1972, $12,000,000 is
being made available, and in 1973 it is projecting grants
totalling $18,000,000. This method of giving foreign aid is
gaining favour. The future success of this program will depend on how agencies such as MCC will respond and with what
responsibility they will administer these additional resources.
Conditions for the acceptance of CIDA funds have been
outlined as follows:
"Each organization that seeks financial assistance from
CIDA for one or more projects in aid of developing countries
must be:
(a) Clearly identifiable as Canadian;
(b) A national or parent body in the case religious
organization not an individual order, parish, chapter or branch;
(c) Operated efficiently to ensure competent execution
of project;
(d) Prepared to provide CIDA with financial statements
indicating its ability to meet its share of the obligations
connected with the project."

(The above information is taken from Special Programs Division Guide for organizations seeking project assistance.)

MCC (Canada) Involvement: Only Canadian agencies can qualify for CIDA funds. Canadian Mennonite interest and financial involvement are taken into direct account in considering each application for a grant. For this reason, MCC (Canada) feels that the time has come to appoint a person to develop and submit project proposals, and to report on them once the projects are underway. This project officer would be primarily a program person, not an administrator. The receipt of development funds from CIDA would free MCC to use its own funding for the placement of personnel. MCC would thus become more of a personnel resource, a direction which should find a positive response from the constituency.

The function of the appointed project officer would be as follows:

(a) To keep MCC fully informed of Canadian government resources, interests, and concerns in development work;

(b) To keep CIDA informed of relevant MCC activities, special interests, and concerns;

(c) To explore, develop and submit projects which would interest CIDA in order to obtain funds earmarked for that purpose (applications would be made in close coordination with MCC's overseas administrators); making helpful material available and generally playing a supportive role.

Since MCC would have several CIDA-supported projects, the project officer's support could legitimately be covered from CIDA funds. On the other hand, there might be compelling reasons for MCC to absorb the cost for such a person, although travel expenses could be included in the total project cost. In either case, the initial outlay would be a relatively small percentage of the total CIDA receipts.

Timing: In 1971 MCC received a total of $129,000 from CIDA. In 1972 we already have received $100,000 for emergency aid to Bangladesh, and we expect to receive an additional $80,000 for development work. No new applications have been submitted this year. With the government's stepping up available funds it would seem to be an opportune time right now to appoint someone to such a desk. There is no doubt that a period of orientation would be necessary. If we wish to receive additional funds during 1973, we will need to make applications early next year. Since most projects are submitted for a defined period, i.e. three to five years, it would make sense to appoint a project officer for a two-to-four year period. At the end of that time, the term could be extended in a realistic way since program trends will be evident by that time. Should funds no longer be available, or should CIDA's policies become unsympathetic to our philosophy of service, curtailment or even cessation

of this kind of program could be enacted quite readily.
Qualifications and Appointment:
   * Intimate understanding of MCC, its philosophy, and
an appreciation of the Mennonite churches
   * Overseas experience in development work, preferably
with MCC
   * Good grasp of basic administrative procedure
   * Experience in working with governmental and related
agencies
   * Basic understanding of rural work and/or primary
industries
   * Canadian citizenship mandatory
   * Christian diplomat and statesman
   Administrative Implications: There are several
factors which will need careful consideration in the creation
of a development desk. The project officer will be working
mainly with overseas programs and local funding agencies,
i.e. CIDA, Oxfam, etc. MCC (Canada)'s interesests need to
be recognized. It must also be borne in mind that the Akron
office has been given responsibility for all activity relating to overseas work. Therefore, the following administrative implications need to be taken into account:
   * It is essential that MCC Akron be primarily involved
in the selection of the candidate.
   * Because he will be part of the MCC (Canada) team,
it is important that MCC (Canada) be tied into the selection
and appointment process.
   * The project officer should be directly responsible
to MCC overseas area directors in project planning, project
missions, advising, and other activities relating to programming.
   * In certain projects, it is conceivable that direct
contact with field personnel will be desirable. Area directors
would be kept fully informed.
   * Should development work not require the full time
of the project officer, MCC (Canada) would then utilize the
balance of his time.
   * On MCC (Canada) work projects, the project officer
would be responsible to the Executive Secretary of MCC (Canada).
   * Financing for a development desk would be the responsibility of MCC (Canada). Programs or budgets would be
charged on a pro rata basis.
   Conclusion: A project officer on the MCC (Canada) staff,
intimately involved with the MCC's international work, will
greatly facilitate interpretation of MCC to the constituency
as well as convey the interests of the Canadian constituency
to our MCC administration. It would strengthen our impact
overseas as well as our inter-constituency relationships.

Insight into the extensive and growing involvement of
MCC (Canada) in many issues of national importance is given
in the ten-year review of its chairman Newton Gingrich.

Reading 64

MCC (Canada) Ten Year Review And Projection. To the MCC
(Canada) Annual Meeting, Edmonton, Alberta, January 11-12, 1974.

It is 1974 and MCC (Canada) is ten years old. At the
Portage Avenue Mennonite Brethren Church, Winnipeg, on December 12-14, 1963 "It was resolved to adopt the name MCC
(Canada)" and approved that "The incoming Executive assume
responsibility to direct the work and to arrange for the
complete takeover of all functions by no later than November
30, 1964." Provincial structures were also proposed using
the MCC prefix.

At the same gathering David P. Neufeld's dream shared
in an April 19-20, 1968 meeting of conference representatives
and Relief and Service agency people at the Sargent Avenue
Mennonite Church, Winnipeg, came to fulfillment. He had projected:

- A simple organization - a common point of contact
                        - a clearing house
                        - accepting responsibility for
                          inter-Mennonite work
- A big organization   - to cut down on overhead
                        - to unify program
                        - to give organizational flexi-
                          bility
- A co-operating organization - with Mennonite Central
                          Committee
                        - retaining the strength of
                          existing organizations
- An independent organization, needing - a united voice
                        - an inter-Mennonite rallying
                          point
                        - an independent immigration
                          program
                        - a limited independent relief
                          program
                        - a strong promotional program

Already on September 25-26, 1959 a conference held at
Winnipeg took action "To study unification of relief and
related programs. Each conference and relief organization
is to reflect on the above and in six months react to the
Historic Peace Church Council of Canada." Not until November 29, 1962 at another gathering was it agreed that the
"Historic Peace Church Council of Canada (HPCCC) representatives
study and explore the establishment of an Inter-Mennonite

Canadian organization to co-ordinate existing Inter-Mennonite
organizations and functions." The name, Canadian Mennonite
Council, was suggested.

When in the December, 1963 meeting an action was approved,
"That the HPCCC be dissolved," a number of other organizations
were implicated. On their own initiative each in due time
disbanded. The main one was the Canadian Mennonite Relief
and Immigrant Council which in 1960 was the result of a
merger between the Canadian Mennonite Board of Colonization
organized in 1922 (incorporated 1925) and the Mennonite Central Relief Committee for Western Canada established in 1940.
The former also had provincial Relief and Immigration Committees, the foundings of which took place in British Columbia
in 1928, in Alberta in 1929, in Saskatchewan in 1942, in
Manitoba in 1928 and Ontarion in 1922. In Ontario was also
the Non-resistant Relief Organization (NRRO), founded in 1917,
and the Historic Peace Church Conference started in 1940.
The latter was an outgrowth of the Peace Committee with participation by the Mennonite, Mennonite Brethren, Brethren in
Christ, and Quaker groups. In the west was also the Canadian
Mennonite Relief Committee organized in 1940 by eight groups
that withdrew from the provincial Relief and Immigration
Committee.

The present facility at 50 Kent Avenue, Kitchener, built
in 1960, was to house the MCC branch office for Canada with •
the provincial organization retaining responsibility for the
property. The clothing depot eventually was administered
via MCC (Canada). The Yarrow, B.C. clothing depot, begun in
1960, was transferred from the Canadian Mennonite Relief and
Immigration Council to MCC (Canada) on September 9-10, 1966
with a value of $20,000. In 1964 the MCC (Canada) office
was established in Winnipeg.

The Annual Meetings for MCC (Canada) were held as
follows:

1965 - February 5-6   - Elmira, Ontario - Mennonite Church
1966 - January 7-8   - Vancouver, British Columbia - First
                        United Mennonite Church
1967 - January 13-14 - Winnipeg, Manitoba - Elmwood Mennonite
1968 - January 13-14 - Saskatoon, Saskatchewan - First Menno-
                        nite Church
1969 - January 10-11 - Calgary, Alberta - Foothills Menno-
                        nite Church
1970 - January 16-17 - Virgil, Ontario - Bethany United
                        Mennonite Church
1971 - January 15-16 - Clearbrook, British Columbia - Menno-
                        nite Brethren Church
1972 - January 14-15 - Steinbach, Manitoba - Mennonite
                        Brethren Church
1973 - January 12-13 - Saskatoon, Saskatchewan - First
                        Mennonite Church

The guest speakers for these meetings were:
1965 - Melvin Loewen; 1966 - Elmer Neufeld; 1967 - Atlee
Beechy; 1968 - Edgar Stoesz; 1969 - Peter Dyck; 1970 - Orrie
Miller & Peter Dyck; 1971 - H. H. Dick; 1972 - Paul Kraybill;
1973 - Returned Workers, with audio-visuals.

Following are some of the developments during these
ten years.

1964 - J. M. Klassen appointed Executive Secretary
     - The C. A. DeFehr & Sons office facility accepted free
       of charge
     - Responsibility accepted for Mennonite Disaster Service
       in Canada
     - Canadian Mennonite Relief and Immigration Council
       office furniture purchased
     - J. M. Klassen visited South America
     - $3,000 given to Friesland Colony in Paraguay
     - Representation to the MCC was finalized
     - Voluntary Service responsibility for Canada was assumed
     - The Peace and Social Concerns Committee along with the
       MCC (Canada) chairman and secretary attended the
       Peace Section Meeting
     - Mennonite Economic Development Associates (MEDA) re-
       presentative appointed to represent the $1,050 shares
       given by Canadian Mennonite Relief and Immigration
       Council

1965 - Assumed responsibility for the Canadian National
       Exhibition, Toronto Peace Booth
     - An exploratory meeting for Mennonite Homes and Hospi-
       tals was arranged
     - Helped sponsor a business ethics seminar in Winnipeg

1966 - Decided not to have a presence at Expo 67 in Montreal
     - planned to send someone to North Vietnam
     - Approved the hiring of an administrative assistant
     - Decided to give the Canadian Mennonite $5,000 (later
       recinded)
     - Publications authorized: Who Are The Mennonites? -
       Frank Epp. Protrait of a Peacemaker - Nick Dick
     - Accepted charter flight responsibility to Mennonite
       World Conference in Amsterdam
     - David P. Neufeld visited Russia
     - Decided to rent office space in the Paris Building
     - Agreed to co-operate with the Centennial Inter-faith
       Committee
     - Joined the Overseas Institute of Canada
     - Daniel Zehr appointed Peace and Service Secretary

1967 - Granted a fund for North Vietnam relief
- Approved a major immigration study
- Encouraged historical societies to produce a History
  of Mennonites in Canada
- Projected a workcamp for the International Peace
  Gardens
- Food for India promotion
- Toronto Service Program plans finalized
- Canadian Mennonite Relief and Immigration Council immi-
  gration records microfilmed
- The chairman attended a Canadian Centennial Service
  in Ottawa
- Nicolas W. Dick was appointed Toronto Service Program
  Director
- Agreed that the MCC (Canada) members attending Menno-
  nite World Conference visit Dr. Landman in Germany
- Became a member of Interfaith Immigration Committee
- Registered for income tax receipt number
- Participated in the inter-church brief to government
  on divorce
- Engaged Larry Kehler for information services
- J. M. Klassen visited South America

1968 - Daniel Zehr appointed Acting Executive Secretary
  during J. M. Klassen's one year leave
- A MCC (Canada) self-study authorized
- More recruitment encouraged
- A questionnaire circulated to pastors regarding peace,
  government witness, etc.
- Funds raised for Middle East program
- J. M. Klassen trip to Korea
- Offered Evangelical Fellowship of Canada constituents
  to process their material aid
- Prepared news release on war taxes and draft resistors
- Peace meeting held at the International Peace Gardens
- Several delegates attended a conference on Church and
  Society
- Pulpit exchange encouraged for Peace Sunday
- Consideration given to immigrants from India
- Applied to external aid for $40,000 for ocean freight
- Combined fund raising for Biafra and Middle East
- Endorsed housing a Baptist group from Russia
- Prepared a Native Peoples' study guide
- Sent a representative to conference on International
  Year for Human Rights
- Authorized a brief and visit to Prime Minister
  Trudeau
- Purchased 9% Menno Travel Service stock for $4,736.
- $10,000 budget approved for North Vietnam

1969 - Kathleen Froese appointed Self Help Co-ordinator
     - Authorized a publication study
     - Agreed to share service and costs for Joerg Isert from
       Germany
     - Daniel Zehr participated in a Middle East Study tour
     - J. M. Klassen trip to South America authorized
     - Arranged for office rental from MCC (Manitoba)
       Ottawa Service Program approved
     - Rejected membership in the Canadian Hunger Foundation
     - Approved Project Bridge Building with Japanese
     - Prepared a brief on poverty
     - Agreed to additional Menno Travel Service shares
       worth $3,600.
     - Regretfully accepted J. M. Klassen's resignation

1970 - Considered an Ottawa Office and a national delegate
       consultation
     - Walter Paetkau hired as Fraser Valley and Vancouver
       Service Director
     - Approved Daniel Zehr leading a Middle East Study tour
     - Daniel Zehr assigned as Executive Secretary
     - David P. Neufeld visited Russia
     - Approved a job description for a Newfoundland Program
       Director
     - Staff asked to investigate Canadian International
       Development Agency (CIDA) funds
     - CBC-TV accepted an MCC minute spot
     - Special Quebec study approved

1971 - Yarrow property transfer to MCC (British Columbia)
       approved when feasible
     - Officers' terms approved for three years, with limit
       of two successive terms
     - Noted the News Brief response encouraging
     - Prime Minister Trudeau contacted regarding families in
       Russia
     - A Buffalo, New York, War Resistors meeting report re-
       ceived
     - Invitation extended to MCC to conduct its annual
       meeting in Canada
     - John Wieler trip to Bangladesh
     - Encouraged Bruce Jutzi to visit China
     - Africa trip approved for Daniel Zehr
     - Appointed a Russia Concerns Committee
     - Accepted membership in a Missionary Health Institute

1972 - A national leadership consultation approved
     - The years of service recognized as rendered by E. J.
       Swalm and C. J. Rempel

- Created a Peace Scholarship fund
- A June meeting held with the Baptists in Toronto
- Became an affinity group for Menno Travel Service
- Requested that MCC utilize professional services for short terms
- Appointed a Mexican Concerns Committee
- Acted to send $1,250 annually to the Conrad Grebel Peace Library for three years
- Gave $3,000 for a Mennonite World Conference film
- Arranged for minute exchange with provincial MCC's
- Decided to have a development desk at Winnipeg
- A statement produced regarding Uganda refugees sent to External Affairs and Immigration
- Considered a membership request by the Bethesda Hutterite Colony
- Daniel Zehr joined a CIDA sponsored trip to India and visited Bangladesh and Nepal
- Ernie Regehr assigned an Arms Industries and Defence Policies study

1973 - $1,500 provided for a Latin America agricultural co-ordinator, when needed
- Guidelines approved for accepting non-church funds, and approved amnesty and Capital Punishment statement
- Recommendations received from the leaders' consultation
- Mennonite Reporter sent to all Canadian Volunteers
- Montreal Service Program plans approved
- Delayed membership in Can Fund
- The office designated as a depository for historical films
- Self Help guidelines approved
- Considered delegate representation to Canadian Catholic Conference as well as the World Peace Congress
- Another leadership consultation planned with conference representatives
- The preparation of an immigration brief to Ottawa approved
- Agreed to projected Peace Literature writing plans
- John Wieler trip to the Sahel of Africa authorized
- First Peace and Social Concerns Committee report received
- Prepared paper on MCC (Canada)'s tenth anniversary
- Dan Zehr trips to Africa and North Vietnam authorized
- Move into larger office facilities approved

During these ten years the following persons served on the executive:
D. P. Neufeld, Ted Freisen, Newton Gingrich - 1964-1974; C. J. Rempel - 1964-1972; E. J. Swalm - 1964, 1966-1971; Harvey Plett - 1964-1968; C. Wilbert Loewen - 1964-1967; J. J. Thiessen - 1964-1966; James Mullet - 1967-1971; J. H.

Unruh - 1968; Peter D. Friesen - 1969; Leonard Freeman - 1970;
John D. Friesen, Jake Harms - 1971; Helen Janzen - 1971-1974;
Leonard Siemens, Hugo Friesen - 1972-1974; Ben Hoeppner - 1972;
Henry Dyck - 1973.

Budget	Actual	Year	Material Aid
$ 83,735.12	$ 104,059.61	1964	$
391,031.18	705,620.54	1965	367,331.95
737,680.00	836,942.49	1966	342,520.05
844,360.00	1,098,509.22	1967	380,998.94
1,089,421.00	1,055,689.63	1968	334,403.40
945,168.00	942,860.27	1969	402,618.70
1,185,857.00	1,149,205.84	1970	456,500.89
1,338,050.00	1,542,041.85	1971	501,332.65
1,387,844.00	1,460,459.60	1972	412,667.50
1,337,866.00		1973	

GENERAL OBSERVATIONS
   - There has been good growth in program, finances and
personnel.
   - There have been mistakes, criticisms, suspicions,
false accusations and limited vision.
   - There has been positive support, encouragement, in-
volvement and wise counsel.
   - Overseas programming via Akron has been a basically
good experience.
   - Personnel processing via Akron has been improved and
in general satisfying.
   - A fair share of the MCC budget and personnel resource
has been supplied.
   - The question of an Ottawa office has been the most
divisive consideration.
   - A major decision that was recinded was the donation
to the Canadian Mennonite.
   - There has been a good relationship with provincial
MCC's.
   - Grass roots involvement has enabled significant
growth.
   - Native people's programs have been too limited.
   - Actual giving has practically always been in excess
of the budget.
   - Material aid remained quite constant the first five
years with a gradual increase until 1971 and then a decline.
   - There was less Canadian programming than some hoped
for.
   - Staff became more involved in overseas work than
earlier envisioned.
   - Conferences have not provided as much guidance as would
be desirable.

- MCC (Canada) has gained respect amongst numerous Canadian agencies.
- MCC (Canada) has also become well accepted in the constituency.
- Closer working relationships with conference mission boards would have been helpful.
- The scripture read at the organizational meeting is still appropriate. Luke 17:5-10.

PROJECTIONS

With that same challenge, where do we go from here? Expectations for MCC (Canada) undoubtedly vary. Permit me to stimulate your vision with some hopes I have.

1. That the Canadian and USA MCC's can become counterparts in all overseas work.

2. That there can be closer co-ordination with mission boards particularly for programs in Canada and perhaps some day there can be unified planning.

3. Hopefully MCC (Canada) or some other agency can become the unifying structure for all inter-Mennonite work in Canada.

4. That numerous outreach ministries can be established in all Canadian provinces.

5. That MCC (Canada) can help build trust between constituent groups.

6. That as Mennonites in Canada we will never lose sight of a wholistic approach to the mission of the church and will increasingly plan to structure accordingly.

7. That as Mennonite groups in Canada we can learn how to dialogue and work with other religious bodies giving a strong witness and learning from them.

8. That the various constituent groups can become a resource to one another, to help work through their differences and find new fellowship and appreciation.

9. To develop creative programs that meet the needs of the day and are not only guided by historical precedence.

10. To help challenge all constituent member churches to utilize their resources to the full in ministering to a needy world.

MCC (Canada) has a future. The structure, programs, methods and even name may be altered. However we have discovered that we need each other, we can help each other and together we can fulfill a ministry which one of us can do alone. The effectiveness for the future will largely depend on how seriously we want to serve together.

Respectfully submitted,

Newton Gingrich
Chairman   *   *   *

A major development in the mid-seventies was the proposal to establish an MCC office in Ottawa. There had been
an "Ottawa presence" for some years in the persons of Frank
H. Epp and voluntary service worker Ernie Dyck, leading to
a formal proposal in January, 1974 by MCC (Canada) director
J. M. Klassen.

Reading 65
Statement Regarding An MCC (Canada) Office In Ottawa, to
the MCC (Canada) Annual Meeting. Edmonton, Alberta,
January 11-12, 1974.

Since the subject of an Ottawa office is not a new
one, it is, perhaps, safe to assume that the members of
MCC (Canada) are familiar with the following documents:
    1. The Executive Committee's report to the MCC
(Canada) Annual Meeting, Clearbrook, B.C., January 15-16, 1971.
    2. The MCC Peace Section Washington Office: A Review,
November, 1972.
    3. The Canadian Council of Churches proposal for an
Ottawa office, March 31, 1969.
    4. Minute 14 of the MCC (Canada) Annual Meeting of
January 14-15, 1972.
    5. Doug Snyder's report on the June 29, 1973 meeting
of the Canadian Council of Churches regarding an Ottawa
Office.
    This paper will seek to present the rationale for an
Ottawa Office based on the belief that individual Christians
and congregations ought to be aware of what the government
of Canada is doing or planning to do and seek to influence
the government to pursue a course of action that most nearly
approaches the biblical role of governments, as God's agents
for the rewarding of those who do good and the punishing of
those who do evil. (Rom. 13).
    Where, at one time, there may have been a basis for
assuming that Canada's laws were built upon the Ten Commandments and that the Christian perspective would be advanced
by the members of parliament, it is now becoming increasingly
evident that Canada is a religiously "neutral" stance. At
the same time the government is moving more and more into
the area of social legislation, a field which lies very
close to the heart of the Christian, and more specifically
the Mennonite, church.
    It is the opinion of this writer that a Christian is
a political figure. The very nature of the democratic process implicate the citizens of the state and make an apolitical
position untenable. The question is not so much whether
or not a Christian is or should be involved in politics but
how this involvement is best expressed and what direction

his influence should take. Some Christians choose the route
of involvement via political parties and seek election to
legislative bodies thereby attempting to influence legislation
and policy. The pros and cons of this type of involvement
is a subject too broad for discussion in this paper, but
the fact remains that even though there are Christians in
government, their views are often tempered by party policies
and constituent pressures. Indeed, Christians in the legis-
latures of our country might be helped if they heard the
voice of the Christian church more clearly!

· The New Testament does not prescribe an Ottawa Office
any more than it prescribes a Sunday School, a Bible college
or a denominational paper. Participation in legislative
processes of governments in Jesus' and Paul's days was not
an option as it is in the Canadian democratic system. To
find the biblical basis for an Ottawa Office we must apply
the clearly visible and timeless principles in the same way
as we applied them to the launching of Sunday Schools, Bible
colleges and denominational papers. For the latter it was
simply the implementation of "teaching them to observe whatsoever I have commanded you", and in the former, "Thy kingdom come, Thy will be done on earth as it is in heaven." Who
will interpret the Lord's will to the legislators of our land
if it is not the Christian church?

The complex problems facing our government do not have
simple solutions. We must not be so naive as to believe that
the church has the expertise to solve all of our country's
problems. But our government is open to and receives signals
from a wide variety of sources on almost every issue. What
a tragedy if the only voices heard on parliament hill are
those of labour, the manufacturing associations and farmers'
unions. The very nature of pressure groups is to seek favour-
able legislation for their own interest group. Who will say,
"Thus saith the Lord" on parliament hill today? Who will
speak on behalf of those who have no spokesman? Mennonites
have, in the course of their history, spoken in Moscow,
Washington and Ottawa when our own lives and destinies were
at stake. The principle of speaking to government has been
an accepted one for many years. Now that we are reasonably
secure, comfortable and accepted by fellow-Canadians, are
we willing to let our voices be heard on issues or for causes
which are not necessarily popular but which are God's will
in heaven and on earth?

The foregoing assumes that the Christian (or Mennonite)
church is united in its views on alternatives and principles
which it could recommend to government as the Christian view.
Unfortunately, this is not the case. It is therefore necessary
to word the mandate given to an Ottawa Office so as to avoid
the possibility of having such an office make unauthorized

pronouncements on behalf of the Mennonite constituency. But
that should not stop us from doing what is possible. There
are major issues on which the Mennonite churches are reasonably
united and on which an Office could give expression accordingly.

Perhaps a more important function of such an Office would
be to feed information to the constituency so that intelli-
gent discussion can take place at the local or regional level
and so that congregations, conferences or other groupings can
be helped to present their viewpoints to government at the
most appropriate level. The Ottawa Office would not decide
what to say on which issue, but rather try to stimulate the
constituency to respond to situations based on valid information and analysis.

This should, however, not minimize the significance of
the personal influence an Ottawa staff would have on politicians
and civil servants in informal relationships. The person
assigned to the Ottawa Office would have to enjoy the confidence of the greater majority of constituent groups to make
the office functional.

FUNCTIONS OF AN OTTAWA OFFICE
The Ottawa Office shall be set up to carry out the
following functions with priority given in the approximate
order of the listings.
A. The Office shall serve as an observer in Ottawa, particularly with reference to developments in the federal government, but also as liaison with other church, welfare and
professional agencies in Ottawa.
1. As an observer, the Office shall seek information
and inform constituent groups on developments in areas affecting
the life and work of the Mennonite and Brethren in Christ
churches.
2. The Office shall analyze and interpret trends which
may affect peace, religious liberty, social welfare, education
and related fields.
3. The Office may interpret by counseling with government officials on spiritual and ethical concerns of the
Mennonite groups as they relate to government programs and
legislation, especially as help is solicited by persons in
government.
C. The Office shall serve as a source of knowledge and expertise on peace and social issues related to government.
1. The Office shall be aware of what issues are being
studied and discussed by the federal government and the implications they may have for interests of the Mennonite churches.
2. The Office shall help the churches to know when presentation of their concerns may be most helpful and shall
help in identifying persons with expertise and competence
on issues involved, such as the services rendered on drafting

legislation affecting conscientious objection to military
service, impingement of government on religious liberties,
etc.
3. The Office shall seek to understand how our history,
understanding and experience with the Biblical teaching on
nonresistance and love may aid the government in better establishing justice and order to restrain and minimize the effects
of evil, and to allow the church to function in obedience to
God and the state.
D. The Office shall provide facilitating services for the
constituent groups.
1. Where groups desire such services as education programs for their constituencies, or aid in participating in
programs conducted by other agencies, the Office shall provide such assistance as it can.
2. Due to its location in Ottawa, the Office may be
called upon to do a variety of tasks, such as picking up
visas, assisting in setting up visits unrelated to official
peace and social concern activities. These functions may be
undertaken so long as they do not detract from other functions
and the costs borne by those benefiting from the services.
3. The Office shall be ready to negotiate extension of
its services to other interests of the churches, such as
missions, education, hospitals and homes, etc.

PERSONNEL AND ADMINISTRATION
The Ottawa Office shall begin initially with the following
personnel and relationship.
A. The personnel will be a director and an office secretary,
the latter only part-time at the beginning.
1. The Director should be a person with a deep interest
in the life and work of the church, preferably with pastoral
experience and/or theological preparation.
2. The Director should be skilled in both oral and
written communication in order to serve in a liaison role
between the churches and government officials.
3. The Director should have sufficient administrative
experience and skill to manage the office and its related
functions.
B. The Office shall be responsible to the MCC (Canada) Executive Committee via the Executive Secretary for policy and
program. An advisory committee shall be appointed by the
Executive Committee to give guidance to the director in the
development of the Office.

PROPOSED FINANCES FOR FIRST YEAR OF OPERATION
Staff allowances and benefits $14,000.00
Office rent 1,500.00

Equipment	
typewriter	350.00
dictating equipment	250.00
gestetner	400.00
photo copier . . . . (rental)	
desks and chair	700.00
filing cabinets	80.00
Supplies	400.00
Light, heat and water	150.00
Postage	175.00
Telephone and Telegraph	200.00
Travel	1,500.00
Miscellaneous	500.00
	$20,205.00

BEGINNING DATE
    The Office shall be established as soon as possible in
1974, on a three year trial basis.

Respectfully submitted,
J. M. Klassen

                    *   *   *

    The MCC (Ottawa) office was established in May, 1975.
Following is the first activities report by William Janzen.

Reading 66
MCC (Ottawa) Office Report No. 1 . . . July 20, 1975.

        MENNONITE CENTRAL COMMITTEE, OTTAWA OFFICE

    Report No. 1 to official advisors - D. Zehr, L. Kehler,
F. Epp, L. Siemens--and other interested persons
                    July 20, 1975

    Mennonite Central Committee's Ottawa Office has been in
operation since May and the structure has begun to take form.
With this report I would like to outline the way it seems
to be developing.

                        I

    A number of specific requests for assistance have come
to this office. These have dealt with a wide range of sub-
jects but they have all been limited in scope. Most often
they have been requests for information. These requests
have related to changes in Soviet laws that might effect the
possibility of emigrating from the Soviet Union, to M.C.C.'s
plans for a food bank, to the extent of Canadian defense

spending, to the legal status of Mennonites coming from Mexico
to Canada, to the current debate on immigration policy, to
the feasibility and procedure for travelling to China, and
the amnesty policy that Canadian governments have taken toward Canadian citizens after wars that Canada has been involved in.

There have also been requests for representation. These
have related to the efforts to deal with the prospective
flooding in northern Manitoba resulting from the hydro development project, and the situation in Korea. This latter request came from a Presbyterian missionary travelling through
Ottawa. There was one request from returning M.C.C. personnel
to arrange a series of meetings with government people. Two
requests asked for assistance in the planning of seminars;
one from a student group and the other for the study of a
specific issue. Several groups have been interested in having
M.C.C. participate in their projects - to help financially,
organizationally or as evidence of broader public support for
their undertakings.

2

In addition to responding to such requests, I have
initiated contact with groups that work in areas where we
will have an ongoing interest. These include the Catholic
Organization for Development and Peace, the Toronto based,
Committee for Justice and Liberty which is closely related
to the Christian Reformed Church, the Canadian Council for
International Co-operation which is made up of over one
hundred non-governmental organizations (M.C.C. being one)
concerned with international development, Gatt-Fly a Toronto
based research and publication organization supported by the
Anglican, Catholic, Lutheran, United and Presbyterian churches
and concerned especially with the trade issue as it relates
to international development, C.U.S.O., Pollution Probe,
the United Nations Association of Canada, and the Grindstone
Island Peace Education Corporation which receives most of its
support from the Quakers.

In meeting with members of these groups I have tried
to learn the nature of their work and also to discover
whether there are areas where some co-operation might be
appropriate. Some instances of co-operation are developing.
For example, we may be co-operating formally in the peace
education effort of the G.I.P.E.C. We have become part of
a very loose group which calls itself "the Canadian Coalition
for a Just Economic Order." This has no formal membership,
budget or secretariat but under the leadership of Gatt-Fly
and the C.C.I.C. it will try to co-ordinate research related
to the "new international economic order" which has been

talked about by numerous leaders including our Prime Minister,
our Minister for External Affairs and the American Secretary
of State. This group will also try to encourage the Canadian
government to adopt certain policy positions at the several
major international meetings that are scheduled to take place
within the next ten months to deal specifically with this
new order.

This matter of co-operating with other groups seems
to be somewhat delicate. I sense a concern that this be
handled with care. In part this caution may derive from our
respect for the integrity of the church, that is, our theology
has always stressed the importance of membership and that our
decisions be made, not by church leaders and spokesmen in
isolation but by the membership. This makes it difficult
for us to become part of groups that would take public positions on which our membership had not been consulted. The
hesitancy may also reflect the desire that some of our other
theological insights not be compromised. Nevertheless, there
are instances when our purpose can be furthered by co-operating
with others and we will need to remain open to such possibilities.

3

The contact with our churches has also made progress.
I have spoken at the Valleyview Mennonite Church in London,
Ontario, the Grace Mennonite Church in Regina, and the Neuan-
lage Mennonite Church near Hague, Saskatchewan. In each case
there has been a good response and eagerness to discuss the
issues. The recent sessions of the Conference of Mennonites
in Canada at Swift Current, Saskatchewan, where I served as
delegate for the Ottawa Mennonite Church, and those of the
Mennonite Brethren Conference in Regina, where I spent one
afternoon have also lent themselves for this purpose. In
both instances the Conference leaders introduced me to the
delegate body and a number of people wanted to become acquainted and discuss particular issues. At Swift Current
I was also asked to help formulate a resolution on the sale
of nuclear reactors by our government.

In these travels, which incidentally have come more
from my association with the Ottawa Mennonite Church than
from this work, I have also taken opportunity to establish
contact with persons from our schools and colleges and those
in professions and occupations that seem particularly relevant for this work.

The contact with the Members of Parliament who are also
members of the churches that form part of Mennonite Central
Committee is also developing. Mr. Jake Epp, and Mr. Dean
Whiteway represent Manitoba constituencies and Mr. William
Andres represents the Lincoln constituency in southern Ontario.

The latter two are serving their first term while Jake Epp
is serving his second. These Parliamentarians are interested
in the development of this work and after meeting with each
one I am fairly optimistic that a good relationship can
develop. They welcome reports about the work of M.C.C. at
home and abroad. Some such reports have already begun to
come into this office on a regular basis. I am now trying
to develop this further by establishing contact with many
Mennonite agencies as well as with others for this purpose,
although I realize that only some of these reports will relate to the concerns of the M.P.'s. I am also trying to obtain copies of position statements of various social issues
that church bodies make from time to time. The M.P.'s have
expressed interest in these too and this office should be
well supplied with them.

I would also like to keep these brethren informed on
some of the issues that come on to M.C.C.'s agenda. Again,
not all of these will relate to their concerns but some will
and since they hold these positions of public trust, communication relating to these issues may be mutually beneficial.

In relating to these M.P.'s, I will have to respect
their independence. Even though they all take their church
membership seriously, they have been called to their particular offices not by M.C.C. but by their constituents. M.C.C.
may from time to time wish to see certain issues promoted,
but we should not automatically assume that our judgement will
correspond with theirs. Of course, respect for the independence of other persons is usually a pre-condition for en-
riching dialogue.

5

The work for the forthcoming months falls into several
categories. The area of international development will
need considerable attention partly because it is such an
important part of M.C.C.'s work, but also because it will
figure prominently on the public agenda. The phrase "new
international economic order" was used by the Commonwealth
Prime Minister's Conference in Jamaica last Spring. In
September there will be a special session of the United
Nations General Assembly to deal with it. The countries belonging to the General Agreement on Tariffs and Trade (GATT)
are also planning to meet. And for the spring the United
Nations Committee on Trade and Development is also planning
a conference. Moreover, the House of Commons Standing Committee on External Affairs and National Defense will be reviewing
the whole Canadian international development effort. The
positions that Canada will take at these international conferences and the policy that will rise out of this Parlia-

mentary review seem to call for some input. Of course, this
is a very complex area. It is not just a matter of giving
more aid in better ways. Nor is it only a matter of opening
our markets to the products of the poorer countries through
changes in the international trading structure. It relates
to the whole of our foreign policy and includes immigration
policy and armament sales as well. Nor can it ignore the
evidence of totalitarianism and disrespect for the individual
person in the poorer countries. We should not think that
economic well-being by itself constitutes the kingdom of God.
The issue is multi-dimensional. It is economic and political,
technical and theological.

The question of military expenditures is receiving more
attention. Some Mennonite people in the United States are
arguing that if it was ever right to withhold our bodies
from military endeavours, then maybe it is now right to withhold our dollars. They are publishing a very informative
little newsletter called God and Caesar and apparently, a
number of United States Congressmen have indicated support
for a bill whereby conscientious objectors could give that
portion of their income tax that goes for military expenditures to a World Peace Tax Fund. Plans are underway for a
conference to study this issue this fall.

I have been invited to participate in this conference
but I have also indicated that I am not eager to press this
issue. Our military structure is very small compared to that
of the United States. It has been decreasing rather than
increasing. Some of its efforts, especially the peace-
keeping operations and rescue work are the kind that I am
willing to pay for. Other reasons could be cited, and I have
done so in my correspondence with those planning the conference. Nevertheless, the issue should not be dismissed too
easily. The world's stockpiles of armaments continue to grow
at a sobering rate and we cannot ignore them. While Canada
has a fairly small defense budget, we do have sizeable armament sales and many of these go to the poorer countries. I
find myself more willing to pursue this aspect than that of
defense spending itself.

Other current issues that I am trying to follow up include capital punishment, abortion, violence in the mass media,
gun control, religious and civil liberties, and the proposed
changes in taxing charities.

6

To deal with these issues will mean devoting considerable
time to research. I am also expected to begin writing, through
church periodicals as well as directly from this office. So
far I have spent a considerable amount of time in reading

for what one might call self-education. The need for this
will continue and these items, together with the time given
to dealing with specific requests, to maintaining contact
with other agencies, and with certain aspects of the legislative process as well as with our churches will mean that
time will have to be budgeted carefully.

7

Finally, I would like to share some thoughts about the
theology of this work as I have worked it through for several
of the sermons that I have given about it. Theologians and
political theorists have worked for centuries on the relation
between church and state and that between religion and politics. No formula was ever really satisfactory. One can
trace the problem all the way to the dispute between Samuel
and Saul in the Old Testament. It was Samuel the religious
authority who appointed Saul, the political authority although Samuel did so with considerable hesitation. Saul was
succeeded by David and in his time the political authority
began appointing the religious authorities. But the political
authority did not keep things going well and some generations
later we hear the religious voices of the prophets calling
the political rulers to change their ways. The relationship between the two remained problematical. It seemed to
defy the solution.

Like other major social questions however, this one too
has its personal counterpart and sometimes a look at this
personal dimension can give us a better perspective on the
larger question. At the personal level we know that Jesus'
most important commandment is that of love. He said it many
times and in many different ways. The letters of St. Paul
hold it forth as the most beautiful and most important part
of life. Unfortunately we also know that this is where we
have most of our personal difficulties. The command of the
Bible is not easily fulfilled. It is a daily struggle. Perfect love seems beyond our reach.

As we work at it in our personal ways, we can I believe,
recognize two common pitfalls. On the one hand our effort
to love others often gives way to a domination of others.
And this is often accompanied by condescension and contempt
as well. The other tendency is that of withdrawing and that
is often accompanied by fear. The love which the New Testament calls for, avoids the tendency to dominate as well as
that of withdrawing.

Since the teaching of love is central to the Bible and
since these two pitfalls seem to be very basic, it should
not surprise us to see the struggle reflected in various
larger settings. Thus, when the Hebrews came into contact

with the Canaanites, the Hebrew religious leaders preached
strongly that they should not mix with the Canaanite peoples.
What were the reasons for this? Why were they to avoid mixing?
No doubt there were many reasons and I have not studied the
situation exhaustively, but I believe one can suggest that
some of these other religions represented the tendencies
mentioned above. Was there not, on the one hand, a pretention
that through certain rituals they could control "the gods"
and thereby dominate the affairs of life and hold their
world in the palm of their hands, and manipulate it for their
own ends? Instead of reverence for life and its Author, man
was at the center. He was everything. And on the other hand,
were there not religions where man was nothing, where he
lived in fear of "the gods", where his whole world was at
the mercy of their whim? In a sense this was a withdrawal
from the invitation of life. The faith for which the religious leaders of Israel were working, carried with it an
attitude to life that was neither one of fear and withdrawal
nor one of arrogant domination. It was one whereby life on
earth was seen as part of the ordered creation of a righteous
and loving God who wanted "to bless all the peoples of the
world," and to have them live, not in arrogance but in dignity, not in fear but in His love.

The dilemma is also reflected in the theologies of
church-state relationships that have been formulated in the
so-called Christian era. The spirit of domination has been
strong. It expressed itself in the medieval claim that
Christians had a divine right to rule; it took a very brutal
form in the large crusades of the eleventh century as well
as those of some smaller groups in the sixteenth; it expressed itself in a more dignified way in the principle
known as "the mandate of the saints to rule" of which some
elements were long embodied in Western constitutions; it is
also reflected in the occasional voice of contemporary church-
men saying, "of course we know best, if only those in power
would ask us." To Mennonites, the spirit of withdrawal is
perhaps better known. Sometimes we have withdrawn for good
reasons, but occasionally it has been perpetuated by fear
and sometimes it has led to an attitude of self-righteous
superiority, a form of mental domination.

It is not for me to criticize all forms of withdrawal.
History shows us too strongly that some of the most profound
truths have come from those who have chosen to withdraw from
certain activities of the larger society. Nor are all forms
of domination undesired. I would rather submit my welfare
to a ruler who had some spiritual sensitivity than to one
who did not. Nevertheless in their negative forms the tendency to dominate and that of withdrawing are deviations from

the central teaching of our faith, "for God so loved the
world..."

In this work I will not try to articulate a refined
church-state theology, although on certain issues that may
be necessary. Of more importance, it seems to me, is that
we see this as an effort to carry further the central teaching
of our faith - to love and to serve the world that we live
in and to make our life redemptive. That is the reason for
this "listening post," for working on international development, for trying to find ways of resolving conflicts peace-
fully, for trying to represent those who need representation,
and so on.

Clearly, the setting up of this office is not a move
towards withdrawal although there is still the possibility
of withdrawing from a variety of encounters for which opportunities arise. And hopefully, the work will not get caught
up in the weakness of domination either, although this too
can come even if only as a mental attitude. May the work be
blessed with courage and humility, imagination and discipline,
and may it serve to carry further the central teaching of
our historic faith.

8

I invite all who read this to consider themselves as
advisors, to comment on the work as outlined, to suggest
general priorities as well as specific directives.

*   *   *

Robert Koop joined the Ottawa office staff in November,
1977. Following is his first report, dated February, 1978.

Reading 67
"Between A Hope And A Hard Word".

Carved into the facade at the top of the building at
63 Sparks Street, Ottawa, are the words, "Bible House".
Likewise on the lintel over the main entrance in iron letters
the words, "Hope Building." Among the varied and impressive
occupants within its walls are the Privy Council of the
Government of Canada, the Advisory Council on the Status
of Women, Reuters News Agency, Readers Digest of Canada, the
United Nations Association of Canada, several law firms and
Mennonite Central Committee. It is not very likely that any
of these organizations, in their decisions to locate here,
were greatly influenced by the names given to the building.
The reasons were most surely of a much more pragmatic orientation. Yet there seems to be something strangely significant
about the fact that an office with the motto, "A Christian

resource for meeting human need" finds itself bracketed by
these two messages in stone and in iron. Coincidental?
Probably. Insignificant? Probably not. The imagery begs
for an exegesis.

In a variety of ways the imagery of those captions reflects the impetus that created the office and the vision toward which it strives. It also reflects a tension. The
office was to be a servant of the churches which established
it; at heart a servant of The Word. It was to seek a measure
of justice where there was no justice and a measure of salvation where there was no salvation; at heart a herald of
Hope. Its mandate was to be informed by faithfulness to the
Word of God and its hope rooted in a hope as sure and as
glorious as the church of Jesus Christ. Still we knew from
the nature of the human heart that vision and reality would
not always coincide.

To be sure, the call to this task is not the exclusive
domain of those who work in this office, or of those who work
within the structures of MCC, or of those within the Mennonite
church. Yet it is a call which becomes highly focused in
those to whom it is extended. In a sense it becomes theirs
alone. It is also a call which is thoroughly directed beyond those called. It is not for their consumption alone.
In fact it ought to be cut from the same cloth as the call
to Abraham to be such a pilgrim that through him the nations
would be blessed. It means that from all sides nothing less
than obedience and faithfulness are demanded. There is nothing
vague in that. What might be vague is whether the Ottawa
Office has clearly heard and faithfully followed. That is
determined, in part, by the shortcomings of those who work
there. The judgement of hearing and the judgement of obedience
needs to be made in part by those who work here and in part
by those who sent us. Finally it is judged in full by Him
who called us all.

That question of what has been done is spoken most
strongly to those to whom the talents have been entrusted.
I am one of them. For that reason I offer this account. It
is meant not only for the consumption of the reader to be
better informed. That would be useful and probably important
but less than adequate. More, it is offered that the reader
might enter into the question and engage in the pilgrimmage
which the author not only faces but cannot avoid. It is to
understand that those in the Ottawa Office and those elsewhere are called to a serious task and that faithfulness
and obedience must be sought together and judged together.

What then does MCC's Ottawa office do? The simplest
answer would be to quote the job description: "to serve as
an observer in Ottawa with reference to developments in the
federal government that relate to ministries and concerns

of MCC (Canada)...to make representation to government...to
assist persons and groups related to the MCC (Canada) constituency to procure legitimate services from the government...
to serve as a source of knowledge and expertise on various
matters related to government....to inform the MCC (Canada)
constituency by reporting, analyzing and commenting on issues,
people and activities related to the federal government, ...
and, to perform such other tasks as may be assigned from
time to time." In the words of one of my friends, while re-
ferring to a research paper he was writing, he called it,
"the world, the universe and then some". In our case that
caricature seems rather apropos. It can be overwhelming
and even immobilizing. Still there is good reason to reread
the job description. It may not be canonical but the exercise is not entirely unlike our rereading of the Bible. It
shows us where we are and where we ought to be. It makes
clear that the task at hand is not of our own creation and
that our shortcomings insist on a good measure of humility.
The vision held before us we hold to be good and true and
noble yet it would be dishonest to say that our work fills
the vision. We hope and pray that in part it does; that
justice will not be stymied and that the Kingdom not delayed.

In more specific terms a good deal of our time continues
to be devoted to the matters of assisting Mexican Mennonites
in establishing their Canadian citizenship. My involvement
in this work remains somewhat peripheral. However, with
Bill now devoting an increasing amount of his time to the
pursuit of a doctoral degree through the halls of acedemia,
that has begun to change. This aspect of our work is not
new and since it has previously been reported on at length
I will not repeat what some of you will understand much
better than I. Suffice it to say that the peculiarities of
each case and the complexities of Canadian citizenship laws
hardly make it a routine task. Sometimes it is more analagous
to a jungle. So it is with much gratutude that I acknowledge
the patience of Bill and two officials in the Citizenship
Branch as they attempt to teach me the way of the jungle and
lead me through it. One takes a certain degree of consolation
from the fact that they also struggle through it. Nevertheless the work is enjoyable and rewarding. Although I do not
have the historical and familial ties to these people as Bill
does one still becomes quickly drawn into a deep respect for
the communities and way of life which they represent and the
desire to create a new life both here and in Mexico. The
agony and the ecstacy are inseparable for them and for us.

My own work has tried to focus more strongly on an aspect
of the initial vision and mandate that always encountered
some difficulty in being realized: "to inform the constituency
by reporting, analyzing and commenting on issues, people

and activities related to the federal government". The problem has not disappeared with my coming. Somehow it seems
that "the other tasks as may be assigned from time to time"
have an uncanny ability to crowd into the centre of one's
desk and demand a higher priority than might appear from their
placement on the job description. Maybe that is how it ought
to be. Many times I believe so. Yet the research and writing
is enjoyable and eagerly done and hopefully worthwhile in
the purpose for which it was intended.

To date only two brief articles have been published although more have been submitted. In part it is a function
of one's own difficulty in producing articles that do more
than simply put ink on paper and in part they are also the
victim of editorial discretion. Undoubtedly it is more the
former than the latter.

The writing, however, does not suffer from a shortage
of material. There is an endless stream of issues that present themselves: Immigration policies, foreign aid, military
expenditure, trade tariffs, disarmament, capital punishment,
national unity, and foreign and domestic policy on a host
of issues. All of them deserve the response of the gospel
of Jesus Christ. Indeed the evil and injustice of some demand
a response before "tomorrow". They cannot be left on the
back burner much longer.

A variety of other activities have also called for involvement since my coming here last November. Included are
participation in a number of meetings and conferences.

In November, with John Wieler and Niel Reimer from
Akron, I attended three days of consultation between CIDA and
various non-governmental organizations. It was a quick and
good introduction to the work of NGO's overseas and the
government's role in those efforts.

In December and January three sets of MCC meetings were
attended in Winnipeg and Kitchener. Again the value was much
to my own benefit as I met fellow MCC'ers, board and executive members and learned more about the work of my colleagues.
The orientation begun in Akron was not completed there.

Other meetings have included the Canadian Council of
Church's Commission on Canadian Affairs in Toronto to map out
a strategy for the coming year. Future discussions were to
include such areas as French/English relations, capital punishment and prison reform. In Ottawa there have been several
meetings with the Canadian Council for International Cooperation
to discuss such varied topics as CIDA-NGO relations, NGO efforts in the larger picture of Canada's response to the world
food supply, and South-east Asian refugees. Although not
extensive, MCC has maintained links, some formal, some less
formal with both the CCC and CCIC.

Efforts have also been made in several small representations to Otto Lang's office concerning MCC's Food Bank to gain further clarity concerning the possibility of permitting wheat contributions outside of the quota systems. The continuing answer is that such a request cannot be granted. Considerable effort has also gone into clarifying family allowance eligibility for MCC personnel going overseas, as well as dealing with one specific application from Bangladesh. It seems that the procedures involved may finally be resolved although they are not quite as simple as we had hoped. In essence each application will need to be evaluated on its own merits. MCC cannot be given an "across the board" approval for all its personnel.

More recently a day was spent at the University of Ottawa as part of their International Week activities. The purpose was to present the work of NGO's in third world development to university students. In essence it meant providing an information table. Although not a great deal of interest was shown in the work of MCC there was much interest in what NGO's, more broadly, are doing overseas. Some inquiries were made at our table but it is clear that the strongest representation we have on campus is through Anne Garber, a student who has been in Zaire with COM-AIMM and is presently considering service with MCC. She has done a great deal to interest a number of students in voluntary service, some of whom have applied to MCC. One is very thankful for such a sustained and capable presence.

Various other activities have included a meeting with a Cambodian refugee, Pin Yathay, who was touring North America both to inform people of the dire plight of his fellow countrymen and to organize support for them; attending lectures by William Epstein, formerly with the UN and an expert on disarmament, by Gerald Vandezande of the Committee of Justice and Liberty during the recent Ten Days for Development activities and by Susan George and Gonzolo Arroyo both food and development experts involved as guest speakers during the Ten Days programme. There have also been several occasions to meet with M.P.'s and the interviewing of a Hatian couple interested in service with MCC.

Perhaps one of the more interesting and continuing activities of the Ottawa Office, is a fortnightly noon meeting with a number of individuals from the Ottawa Mennonite Church. The purpose is to discuss a variety of public affairs issues and the way in which Christians ought to relate to the federal government. Topics have included federal options in the face of an expected Quebec referendum on independence, the merits of minority government, Mennonites in politics, Canada's foreign aid policy, and disarmament. The latter has resulted in a letter addressed to the Prime Minister expressing our concerns and hoped for government action at the

special session of the UN on disarmament this spring. It
continues to be of considerable value to meet with these
people and to consider again the nature of our work in Ottawa.
The activities described here have hopefully given something of a picture of the continuing work of MCC's Ottawa
office. In the future there will probably be an increasing
involvement in Native concerns through contacts with government officials and national native organizations in Ottawa.
Similarly with offender ministries. To these involvements
I look forward with some interest. There will also be many
tasks which now cannot be foreseen but which will also demand our attention.

To become involved in all the things we would like to,
or ought to, seems, in many ways, to be beyond our reach.
One is often torn between a little involvement in many things
and much involvement in a few. It is not always easy to decide which way to turn since each has its advantages and
disadvantages. Sometimes one feels like a kind of Jack-
of-all-trades and master of none.

Yet the answer is not simply one of picking and choosing
those areas in which to apply ourselves. The variety of requests which come to the office can hardly be expected to
cease. Indeed their number will probably increase. Our
response to some can be delayed for a time but they cannot
be ignored forever. Some do not even permit a delay. Sooner
or later an answer of some kind must be given to all of them.
What is regrettable and probably reprehensible is that the
response is sometimes too late, or less than adequate, or
less than what we are capable of. Where we have failed in
obedience to our calling we need to repent.

One final comment. At various times I have heard this
office described as being a prophetic voice to the Canadian
government and to the Mennonite churches. That is undoubtedly
noble company to be associated with and if only a small measure of it is true it will speak much more loudly of the
work of our God than ourselves. To date neither the Kingdom
of God nor Trudeau's just society have been fully realized.
Whether we will be able to consumate either is rather doubt-
ful. Perhaps what is reassuring is that the prophets' faithfulness did not always mean that the justice they sought was
finally achieved.

One thing is clear. The course of history is beyond
the control of even the most faithful of Christians, including MCC's Ottawa office. Our continuation can only be
in prayer and in faith that the work entrusted to us is indeed the work of our Father.

Respectfully submitted,
Robert Koop

:   a small disclaimer - the title of this report was in-
spired by Mark O. Hatfield

*   *   *

A brief review of MCC (Canada) Ottawa office activities
during 1978 was submitted to the January, 1979 Annual Meeting
by William Janzen.

Reading 68
Annual Report for 1978 . . . Calgary, January 19-20, 1979.

This report contains 1) an overview of the work that
was done this past year, 2) a brief note about the structure
and 3) some comments about the future.

The pattern of work in the Ottawa Office in 1978 was
similar to that of preceeding years. There was no single
particularly outstanding project. Instead there were a
variety of small ones.

A brief asking that the new Constitution of Canada include a clause for the protection of conscientious objectors
was prepared and submitted to the Parliamentary committee
working on the constitution.

Another brief was prepared for the Canadian Consultative
Council on Multiculturalism. In fact, there were two briefs.
The main one was submitted to a conference of national organizations held in Ottawa late in October. A smaller one,
dealing with a more specific issue, was prepared for a regional conference of the Council, held in London, Ontario,
in April.

An intervention was made in regard to a circular from
the Revenue Department which seemed to say that charitable
institutions would have to refrain from certain kinds of
activities or else lose their tax exempt status. When the
circular came to our attention we arranged to meet with the
officials in charge. Our report from that meeting, which
received considerably more public attention than we expected,
played a part in the government's decison to withdraw the
circular. The issue however, is not resolved yet.

A considerable amount of work was done to determine
how foreign service under MCC affects the eligibility of
Canadian citizens for Family Allowance and Pensions. Several
specific cases have been resolved. But the general question
is still not settled.

Quite a lot of Kanadier work was done. Some time was
given to the service program in southern Ontario. Numerous
specific cases, originating from Mexico, the United States
and Canada's five western-most provinces, were dealt with.
Efforts were also made to negotiate further improvements in
the system for handling the specific cases.

There were also a number of small requests for Ombudsman-type services. These related to things like the cutback
in the government's prison chaplaincy program, laws regarding
conscientious objection to labour unions, immigration cases
from Germany, MCC's work in other countries, Mennonite interest
in Amnesty International, documentation needed by MCC and
other Mennonite personnel to go to their places of service,
the existence and availability of Canadian technology to
clear the farming fields of Laos of unexploded amunition, etc.

Contact was maintained with certain people and organizations including, the Canadian Council for International Co-
operation, The Commission on Canadian Affairs of the Canadian
Council of Churches, several Parliamentarians and civil servants. Some visitors were received. Among these were Don
Morton who sought support for South African "draft-dodgers",
Scott Carmichael who sought support for the protection of
some new religious groups, Otto Buchsbaum who sought support
for his campaign against the development of nuclear technology, and David Taylor who sought support for political
prisoners in Thailand.

Various things were done at the request of other port-
folios of MCC (Canada). In some instances meetings were
arranged for them. This was the case with Murray and Linda
Hiebert whose story about Laos and southeast Asia needed to
be heard by certain officials. A number of meetings of governmental and non-governmental organizations were attended
on behalf of other MCC people. Inquiries were made for
them regarding things like the possible reinstitution of
capital punishment, Canada's food policy, certain international
armament transactions. Some Ottawa applicants for MCC work
were interviewed on behalf of the Personnel Office. Some
investigations were done on behalf of Mennonite Disaster
Service etc.

Fifteen articles were written for Mennonite newspapers
on topics like militarism, freedom for religion, abortion,
multiculturalism, multi-national corporations. Most of
these were written by Robert Koop and most, but not all,
were carried in one paper or another.

The structure inside the Office was somewhat different
this year partly because for the first time there was a
Voluntary Service worker and partly because I was out for
half of the time working on my thesis. On the whole things
worked out well although in hindsight I can see that occasionally the eagerness to get back to the thesis meant that
certain things were done too hurriedly and the quality
suffered. I would like to acknowledge, with gratitude, the
good work of Bob Koop, the VS Assistant and Frieda Enns, the
Secretary. Without them things at the Office could have become uncomfortably complex. Late in the year temporary ap-

proval was received for a part-time arrangement with Don
Friesen, Minister at the Ottawa Mennonite Church, whereby
he can do a small amount of writing for the Office on a contract basis.

The future of work at the Ottawa Office, if MCC (Canada)
votes to continue it, will probably be a mixture of the known
and the unknown. It is likely that there will always be
calls for various Ombudsman-type services. The Kanadier work,
which was substantially less in 1978 than in 1977 will not
vanish completely. It will continue to call for a measure
of attention. Opportunities for making formal submissions
regarding our concerns to governmental and non-governmental
organizations can be expected to appear from time to time.
And then there is the on-going need to study and write about
the many developments on the public agenda that relate to
MCC's interest in peace, justice, and development. With
the increased staff time, which for the first time will
amount to two full-time people, it should be possible to do
somewhat more of this.

Respectfully submitted
William Janzen

*   *   *

MCC (Canada) activities continued to grow at many levels
due, in part, to strong provincial organizations. The idea
of an "Ottawa Presence" as already seen, began in 1971; guiding principles for a Peace and Social Concerns Committee
were adopted in 1974; the Mennonite Voluntary Service program
underwent a twenty year review in 1975; the responsibilities
of MDS (Canada-Region V) were spelled out in September, 1976.
Ministries to native Canadians, to Mennonite immigrants from
Mexico, to offenders, and other services were initiated. Unique among Mennonites, and reminiscent of Joseph's work in
Egypt of old, has been the Food Bank which was established in
1977.

Reading 69
February 28, 1977. The Food Bank of MCC (Canada).

Mennonite Central Committee (Canada) is the relief and
service agency of Mennonite and Brethren-in-Christ churches.
Its interest in setting up a food banking system comes from
a number of factors. First, like many others involved in
international relief and development work, it believes that
the idea of food banking can be an important part of a more
general response to the world's food shortages. Secondly,
in discussing the idea with its supporting constituency,
which numbers about 180,000 according to the 1971 Canadian

census and which is deeply rooted in agriculture, it discovered strong support for the idea. And thirdly, through
its international relief and development work, which began
over fifty years ago and which currently operates in over
thirty countries with several hundred Canadian personnel, it
has learned directly about the nature of food needs and about
ways of responding effectively to those needs. The absence
of structures at the national and international level which
are designed to provide stability in the food supply was an
additional motivation.

For these reasons, Mennonite Central Committee (Canada)
proposes to set up a food banking system. However, in view
of the limits of MCC's constituency in Canada and of its programs overseas and since there is relatively little experience
with the working of this concept, it will have to be undertaken in modest proportions. Accordingly, MCC (Canada) proposes that the Food Bank deal only in wheat, that it be set
up for a five-year trial period, that during this period it
accept no more than four and one-half million bushels altogether and hold no more than two million bushels in storage
at any one time. Also, in procuring the wheat it would remain
heavily dependent on the normal grain handling procedures.
The Canadian Wheat Board would assume control of the wheat
at the country elevators in the usual way. It would then make
the wheat available to the Food Bank either for storage or
for immediate international delivery.

The arrangements for its international delivery would
be made by the Food Bank and it would also be responsible for
ensuring its distribution to the people in need. But it would
not set up its own distribution systems in foreign countries.
For this it would be dependent on the international programs
of MCC or on those of other agencies or organizations whose
purposes are compatible with those of MCC with whom it might
make arrangements from time to time.

Although modest in size and operational structure, it
would be a way of working towards several important goals.
First, it would provide a channel whereby wheat producers in
MCC's supporting constituency could make wheat available for
MCC's international relief and development work. By thus
setting up an additional channel for responding to human need
it would increase the resourcefulness of MCC's constituency.
Secondly, it would mean that wheat would go through the various stages from production to distribution, not on the basis
of its monetary value but in response to human need. In doing
so it would give the producer an additional reason for growing
wheat and take off its price tag for those who can not pay.
Thirdly, by building up a reserve, it would increase the
capacity of MCC's programs and those of other agencies and
organizations for responding to diverse situations of need.

Finally, through the power of example and the experience gained
from putting this idea into practice, it will hopefully be
a stimulant to the legislators, planners and administrators
to solve the dilemma of fluctuating food supply and prices
on a more global scale.

If the Food Bank becomes operational and succeeds in its
aim of providing food in emergency situations and stimulating
local food production in developmental situations, it may
lead to a larger food banking system. However, even if a
larger one would appear, the long range solutions to world
food shortages lie not with importing more food, but must be
integrated with efforts to improve the production, storage,
and internal distribution of food within those countries where
food shortages occur.

After studying these goals and purposes in the context
of the existing grain handling mechanisms, financial structures
and distribution systems in foreign countries, it seems that
the following outline may be the most feasible. Therefore,
in general terms we propose:

A. GENERAL DIMENSIONS

The Food Bank of MCC (Canada), hereinafter known as the
Food Bank, will operate for a five-year trial period, during
which time it will procure up to a maximum of 4,500,000
bushels. Wheat will be the only commodity held in storage
during this period, and the amount of wheat held in storage
will be limited to a maximum of 2,000,000 bushels at any
point in time.

B. RELATIONS WITH THE FARMER

Mechanisms will be developed which allow for the widest
range of responses by the farmer in his capacity as a grain
producer. These could include but are not necessarily limited
to the following:

-Donations based on deliveries of wheat or other board
grains to his local elevator and from within this quota.

-Donations based on income from the sale of non-board
grains or other situations where the quota does not apply.

-Donations resulting from special programs negotiated
by the Food Bank and the Wheat Board such as the delivery of
above-quota grain to designated locations.

Farmers will be encouraged to plan their participation
in the Food Bank on a regular basis by designating a portion
of future crops for the Food Bank. This could be an on acre-
age or quantity basis, and limited to situations where the
quota or geography will not be a serious impediment to delivery.

The Food Bank will send each participating farmer an
official receipt equal to the cash value of grain he has donated which is valid for income tax purposes.

C. RELATIONS WITH THE CANADIAN WHEAT BOARD

The Wheat Board has agreed to sell the Food Bank the quantity of wheat represented by the value of the farmer's donations and the additional grant from Canadian International Development Agency (CIDA). The wheat will be purchased at a designated port and held in storage by the Wheat Board on behalf of the Food Bank. The Food Bank will pay the Wheat Board for storage, handling and other authorized services that the Wheat Board may provide.

D. INTERNATIONAL DISTRIBUTION

The Food Bank Board of Directors has the authority and responsibility to plan for the allocation of the wheat and to arrange for transport to the nearest port. MCC, in the form of its international organization, will have the prime responsibility for advance planning, designation of specific situations, and the supervision of programs. The Food Bank intends to cooperate with other organizations in the distribution process where the purposes of the agency are compatible with MCC and there is a capacity to utilize food supplies effectively.

The major portion of the wheat is expected to be used in emergency situations arising out of both natural and manmade disasters. A significant portion of the wheat will be used in food deficient areas to supplement regular development programs designed to stimulate food production. The Food Bank will work with the programs of MCC, and with those of other agencies and organizations whose purposes are compatible with those of MCC, to facilitate the effective integration of Food Bank wheat into development programs.

E. ADMINISTRATION

MCC (Canada) will appoint a Food Bank Board of Directors which should include persons with experience in or understanding of the primary producers, the grain handling industry and the distribution of food in emergency and developmental situations. This Board is responsible to MCC (Canada) for its general guidelines.

MCC (Canada) will further appoint an Executive Director for the Food Bank on the recommendation of the Food Bank Board of Directors.

The Food Bank Board of Directors have the authority to enter into various other agreements with agencies and personnel whose purposes are compatible with those of MCC, including:

a) the hiring of personnel as needed and

b) the appointment of local Food Bank agents to work on a voluntary basis in farming communities in Canada to enlist the cooperation of farmers and to facilitate the work of the Food Bank.

F. FUNDING

MCC (Canada) will contribute to the salary of the Executive Director of the Food Bank and to such other administration costs as may from time to time be agreed to.

The Canadian International Development Agency (CIDA) will provide additional funds related to the participation of the farmer for the purpose of purchasing wheat as well as providing for the costs of storage, ocean shipping and administration.

DATE DUE

NOV 8 1980	DEC 0 1 1997	
APR _ _ 1981	MAR 2 8 1999	
APR 1 4 1996	JUL 0 9 2007	
MAY 4 1981	JAN 0 5 2009	
DEC 7 1981		
MAR 2 8 1982	APR 1 1 2020	
APR 1 1 1982		
MAR 1 2 1982		
APR 2 4 1985		
NOV 1 5 1986		
1-4-84		
APR 1 8 1990		
8 1990		
NOV 2 8 1990		
3-14-92		
NOV 2 1 1994		
2·20·95		
OCT 1 9 1997